2.95

Practical Prayer

Derek Prime

Christian Focus Publications Ltd

*All Scripture quotations are from
the New International Version,
published by
Hodder and Stoughton.*

© 1985 Derek Prime

ISBN 1 871676 517

Published by
Christian Focus Publications Ltd,
Geanies House, Fearn, Ross-shire,
IV20 1TW, Scotland, Great Britain.

CONTENTS

Introduction

'Why pray at all?' Behind that basic question there's often the thought, 'Why does an all-loving and all-knowing God want us to pray anyway? If He knows our needs, and wants to meet them, why does He require us to ask Him to do so?'

We obtain some possible explanation if we consider our relationship to our own parents or children. Parents frequently know what their young children require before they ask. They delight in their children asking them nevertheless, so that they may have the pleasure of granting their requests. Giving and receiving mark out and enrich meaningful relationships. Sometimes we're in a position to give, at other times we have to be on the receiving end. Love and fellowship grow as dependence is recognised by one person, and care is demonstrated by another.

We're dependent upon God for everything, and God delights to meet our needs. Some He supplies on a daily basis without our ever asking Him. Others He provides as we deliberately lay them before Him. We find the primary answer to the question, 'Why pray?' in man's fundamental relationship as a creature to God the Creator - it's one of dependence. And it's a dependence which reflects an essential part of man's unique creation by God - man was created to have fellowship with God.

There are other ways of trying to answer the question, 'Why pray?' There's an unfathomable mystery about our Lord Jesus Christ, the Son of God, becoming man, and taking our human flesh upon Him. The Lord Jesus Christ, in His sinless humanity, shows us what we ought to be like - and what man, in his original state, was like. And here's a significant fact: *Jesus prayed* . Mark records what was clearly Jesus' daily routine: 'Very early in the morning,

5

while it was still dark, Jesus got up, left the house and went off to a solitary place, where he prayed' (Mark 1: 35). Gethsemane witnessed the greatest crisis of Jesus' obedience to the Father's will as He contemplated the Cross when it was just a matter of hours away - *and He prayed* (Luke 22: 41-44). The letter to the Hebrews pinpoints the crucial place prayer occupied in His life: 'During the days of Jesus' life on earth, he offered up prayers and petitions with loud cries and tears to the one who could save him from death...' (Hebrews 5: 7). Since the Lord Jesus is my example in everything, I too should maintain prayer as one of the basic activities of my daily life.

The Lord Jesus prayed because He knew that it was His Father's will and delight that He should do so. The Bible is full of promises and encouragements to pray. The problem isn't in finding the promises, but in grasping all of them and entering into the good of them.

Although I may not be able to answer adequately the question as to *why* God wants me to pray, it's a general principle of Christian experience that I should be guided by what I do know rather than by what I don't! I *do* know that my heavenly Father wants me to pray, and that He delights in my prayers. My Saviour, my supreme Example, encourages me to pray, as do all my heavenly Father's promises. A principal activity of the Holy Spirit - the gift of the Father and the Son to me - is to assist me in prayer.

1
Defining Prayer

Prayer isn't simply *a* most important activity - it's *the* most important. There's no other similar activity upon which every other activity in the Christian life depends. As my pulse is one of the primary indications of my physical life, so my praying is one of the principal proofs of my spiritual life.

Significantly, the Bible doesn't provide a comprehensive definition of prayer. Prayer is beyond definition in the same way that any important relationship with another person is. Personal relationships are always more meaningful than we can express in words, and this is uniquely the case when the One with whom we have this special relationship is the Infinite God! Nevertheless the attempt to define prayer is helpful if we do so to ensure that we enter fully into this tremendous privilege.

Starting points

Prayer is an activity of the soul or spirit

Sometimes the endeavour is made to distinguish between 'soul' and 'spirit'. From the point of view of prayer there's little profit in doing so, since the two words are used interchangeably in the Bible.

When Mary voiced her praise and prayer to God, in what we know as the Magnificat, she began, 'My *soul* praises the Lord and my *spirit* rejoices in God my Saviour...' (Luke 1: 46, 47). The soul (or spirit) is the seat and centre of our spiritual life, in all its varied aspects. Capable as it is of receiving God's salvation and sharing in God's very nature, nothing we possess is more precious. It's no surprise, therefore, that the Lord Jesus is described as 'the Shepherd and Overseer' of our souls. As such He laid down His life for us, His sheep (John 10: 15), bearing our sins in His body on the tree (1 Peter 2: 24), making it possible for our souls to be cleansed and then to be made alive to God.

The success or failure of our spiritual life hinges largely on our appreciation of the soul's value. Since prayer is an activity of the soul, we won't appreciate prayer very much if we don't value our soul's well-being - it's as basic as that. When God the Father and God the Son come to live with us by God the Holy Spirit residing within us - and this is what new birth involves -our soul (or spirit) is God's chosen dwelling-place. The psalmist had it right when he wrote, 'My *soul* thirsts for God, for the living God. When can I go and meet with God?'(Ps.42:2).

Prayer is a response to God's initiative

Whenever we appreciate God's greatness and glory, it seems presumptuous even to think of trying to approach Him. But the glorious truth the Bible proclaims is that God Himself has taken the initiative. David's testimony was, 'To you, O my heart, he has said, "Seek my face!"' (Psalm 27: 8, see NIV footnote). God's supreme initiative was the Cross of our Lord Jesus Christ. Without the Cross and what it achieved, we wouldn't have any assurance that prayer is heard.

Men and women in the Old Testament period - like David whom we've already mentioned - understood the need for atonement. The duly appointed animal sacrifices they offered couldn't take away their sin, but their offerings were accepted by God - and counted as effective - on the basis of that one great and final atoning sacrifice which our Lord Jesus Christ was going to offer for the sins of the whole world. This amazing truth explains why they could pray with something approaching the confidence we may know through our Lord Jesus Christ. They prayed - like us - because they had the assurance that God wanted them to do so, and had made it possible.

Prayer is an expression of God's intimate friendship
Job summed up his relationship with God in this manner (Job 29: 4). Prayer isn't all talking. It's often listening. As we pour out our heart to God, and wait before Him, we may often discern the still small voice of His Spirit speaking to our conscience or stirring us up to appropriate actions or attitudes. More important still, God may provide a new perspective upon a situation - His own. David testified, 'The Lord confides in those who fear him; he makes his covenant known to them' (Psalm 25: 14).

God's friendship is so real that we can share *everything* with Him with no fear of ever being let down. We may sometimes share with our best friends only to regret afterwards that we gave such complete confidences. But never so with God.

Prayer is pouring out our hearts to God
The pouring out of the heart expresses the thought of spontaneous and complete unburdening, of prayer marked by feeling, earnestness and sincerity (Psalm 62: 8; Lamentations 2: 19). It may be the pouring out of joys and praise on the one hand, or groanings (Job 3: 24), troubled thoughts (Psalm 142: 2) and the like on the other.

To pour out our hearts is to unburden our cares completely upon God by telling Him everything as we can to no one else. Hannah found this. Deeply troubled by great anguish and grief, she poured out her soul to the Lord and found extraordinary relief and deliverance by this means (1 Samuel 1: 15, 16).

Have in your mind's eye two glasses: one's empty, and the other's full of water. I then take the one that's full of water and I pour all that's in it into the one that previously was empty. As we pour out our hearts before God like water we completely transfer our cares, our anxieties and our needs to Him - and that's what He wants. We're to empty our hearts before Him of everything that concerns and troubles us. We're to have no 'hang-ups' about telling God *everything* . This lovely aspect of prayer reminds us of the intimacy of friendship, the freedom we may enjoy before our heavenly Father. It's the opposite of bottling things up inside. Sadly we can put a lock on our hearts, and then prayer ceases to be free and spontaneous.

Prayer is being with God

I can recall occasions, when our children were younger and of pre-school age, when there would be a knock at my study-door, or a little head would be poked round the door. 'Yes, what do you want?' I would ask. 'Just to be with you, Daddy!' would be the irresistible reply. No matter how busy I was, I couldn't decline! I look back to those moments with immense pleasure. Amazingly, our heavenly Father delights in our coming to Him in prayer, just to be with Him - not for what we want from Him but simply that we want Him for Himself.

Prayer is communing with God

To commune is to confer and to share. 'Fellowshipping' is a more contemporary way of expressing it. 'Our fellowship is with the Father and with his Son, Jesus Christ' (1 John 1:3). Broken fellowship once summed up the record of our relationship with God but fellowship has been restored.

We may talk to God now, and share His company. That talking takes many forms. We may tell Him how aware we are of His greatness and glory - that's *adoration*. We may express to Him how much we appreciate His goodness to us - that's *thanksgiving.* We'll continually feel the need to tell Him of our sorrow for our sins - that's *confession.* We'll share with Him our personal needs, and our urgent concern for others - that's *prayer, supplication* and *intercession*. We may plead with Him about specific difficulties and receive His answer. Paul records such a situation in his own life: 'There was given me a thorn in my flesh, a messenger of Satan, to torment me. Three times I pleaded with the Lord to take it away from me. But he said to me, "My grace is sufficient for you, for my power is made perfect in weakness"' (2 Corinthians 12: 7-9). Such experiences are most personal, and memorable.

Prayer is all about access to God

'Come near to God and he will come near to you', is a reassuring promise (James 4: 8). Fundamental to our whole understanding of prayer is the basic truth that before there can be access to God there must be peace with God. Peace could be brought about for us only by the blood of Jesus Christ. As Paul puts it: 'Since we have been justified through faith, we have peace with God through our Lord Jesus Christ, through whom we have gained access by faith into this grace in which we now stand' (Romans 5: 1,2). The Lord Jesus is the sole means of access to the Father for both Jew and Gentile: 'For through him we both have access to the Father by one Spirit' (Ephesians 2: 18). This thought of the Lord Jesus being the secret of our access to God is expressed very powerfully, though simply, in the Lord Jesus calling Himself the door or gate of the sheepfold (John 10: 7). There's only one door into God's presence - Jesus Christ, God's Son and our Saviour.

The idea behind the word 'access' is that of an introduction into the presence-chamber of a monarch. In prayer we come before the King of kings, and the One who introduces us is our Lord Jesus Christ. We mustn't allow our concern to use the right words or to follow the proper 'mechanics' of prayer to obscure the sheer wonder and delight of our free access to God through the Lord Jesus.

The New Testament stresses the freedom and boldness with which we may come to God. 'In him and through faith in him we may approach God with freedom and confidence' (Ephesians 3: 12; cf Hebrews 4: 16; 10: 19; 1 John 5: 14). Being a Christian should be synonymous with confident access to God. No human father wants his children to be uncertain of their access to him and of his welcome. How much more is this so with our heavenly Father!

Prayer may express itself in silence before God

Different situations, feelings and emotions make silence appropriate, and we won't always know why. We may feel the need to come into God's presence, but not know what to say. We can't always pray to order. We may be lost for words. We shouldn't be anxious about this, since prayer is the business of the heart more than of the tongue, and God reads our heart as easily as He hears the words of our lips.

There's the silence of confusion , when the storms of life seem to threaten us with disaster, and all we can say is, 'Lord, Your will be done!' and then remain quietly before Him until His peace fills our soul, so that we may go out to face the storms with our strength renewed.

There's the silence of confession, when we've been found out by God (as David once was - see 2 Samuel 12: 7) and we don't feel that it's enough simply to say, 'Lord, I have sinned...' but we need to wait before Him silently in penitence until we're sure that our repentance is genuine and that His forgiveness has been extended to us once again in all its completeness.

There's the silence of worship and praise, when we've caught a fresh glimpse of God's glory in the face of our Lord Jesus Christ, and we're filled with inexpressible joy. One night George Whitefield, the evangelist, wrote in his diary (Wednesday 9th May 1739): 'God was pleased to pour into my soul a great spirit of supplication, and a sense of His free distinguishing mercies so filled me with love, humility, and joy, and holy confusion, that I could at last only pour out my heart before Him in an awful silence. It was so full that I could not well speak. Oh the happiness of communion with God!'

Silence may be prompted by a variety of other reasons. While the Holy Spirit may be depended upon to interpret the wordless prayers of our hearts to the Father, our silence may also give God the opportunity He wants to speak to us. Sometimes we may be so busy doing all the talking that we don't give ourselves the opportunity to listen to God.

Prayer involves waiting upon God

Waiting upon God is a familiar expression in the book of Psalms. An obvious and important part of waiting upon God is being still before Him in quiet meditation; as David in one of his songs says, 'I have stilled and quietened my soul; like a weaned child with its mother, like a weaned child is my soul within me' (Psalm 131: 2).

Sometimes to wait upon God is to make our requests to Him, and then to wait quietly in His presence with the confident expectation that He will act at the right time: 'I wait for the Lord, my soul waits, and in his word I put my hope' (Psalm 130: 5).

Bible pointers

The Bible expresses the activity we describe as prayer in a number of ways. Each provides a window through which we may see a little more of what prayer is.

Approaching the throne of grace

'Let us then approach the throne of grace with confidence', urges the writer of the letter to the Hebrews, 'so that we may receive mercy and find grace to help us in our time of need' (Hebrews 4. 16). By nature we deserve

God's throne to be one of judgment, where we receive His just punishment for our sins and failures. But through the Lord Jesus' atoning sacrifice, God's righteous wrath has been turned away from us, and God is able to be gracious and kind to us, with no detriment to His justice and holiness. Instead of our having to view God as sitting upon a throne of judgment - as our sins deserve - we are encouraged to picture His throne as a throne of grace. He waits to be gracious to us! There's no limit to what He will do for our good, on account of our spiritual union with His Son, the Lord Jesus. A throne is always a symbol of authority: God delights to *command* blessings and benefits upon us as we come to Him in prayer in His Son's name.

Looking to God (Ezra 8:22; Psalm 34:5)
This expresses the dependence we feel upon God, and the expectations we have of Him such as we have of no one else. It's interesting to watch a hungry baby among a group of adults. His eyes are upon one person only - he looks to his mother! She's the one who can satisfy his need.

Calling upon God's Name (1 Kings 18:24)
This expression emphasises that true prayer is essentially a response to what we know about God Himself, the natural outflow of our knowing Him. God's Name - in Bible language - indicates God's character, His total being, all that He's shown Himself to be. He's promised to be the shield of His people, and calling upon His Name, therefore, may mean asking for His protection. He's revealed His love to us, and prayer - calling upon His Name - may appropriately be our casting ourselves upon His love.

Seeking God (Psalm 34:10)
This idea helpfully pinpoints the consulting factor

which may be part of prayer. Seeking God equals wanting his advice. To seek God is to lay our lives before Him, wanting and accepting His way before He even chooses to show it to us. On numerous occasions we don't clearly know what to do, although, so far as we can judge, we want to do only what is right. To seek God is to lay our whole situation before Him, wanting to obtain the insight which He can give to enable us to do the right thing.

Seeking God's face (Psalm 27:8)

This is another delightful Old Testament description of prayer, found most of all in the book of Psalms. Physical sight isn't what is meant, but the seeing of God with the inward eye, which is an anticipation of what's before us in a new and wonderful way in the life to come.

The verb from which the noun 'face' comes means to turn towards someone, to pay attention to him or her. A person's face identifies him to us, and often reflects his feelings, attitudes and sentiments. To seek God's face, therefore, is to come into God's presence with the deliberate purpose of communicating with Him. Let's illustrate this by means of an opposite. Probably we've all known what it is to give thanks for our food before a meal, or to pray the Lord's Prayer together with others, and then to wonder afterwards whether or not we've prayed. Plainly that's the opposite of deliberately and genuinely seeking God's face.

Imagine going into a crowded room in order to establish contact with a friend to enlist his assistance. You know that if you can catch his eye - seek his face - he'll get your message and come to your aid. As you see him in the room, you'll keep looking his way until he sees you, until you see him turn his face towards you. And then you'll know that you've been successful. To seek God's face is to be occupied with God's Person before we start asking Him for anything, and then not to stop seeking Him until we know that His face is turned towards us, and that our requests are received by Him with pleasure. It's no surprise that seeking God's face is a key secret of radiance (Psalm 34: 5).

Top of the list

However we define prayer, at the top of the list we have to put prayer as *asking* . 'Ask and it will be given to you', the Lord Jesus promises, 'seek and you will find; knock and the door will be opened to you. For everyone who asks receives; he who seeks finds; and to him who knocks, the door will be opened' (Matthew 7: 7, 8).

Prayer involves making requests to God (Philippians 4: 6). In prayer we acknowledge our own impotence and deficiencies, and we ask God to do what we can't do for ourselves. James gives the example of the need we have of wisdom for daily living. Trials and difficulties are an inevitable feature of life, and it's important to react in a Christian manner so that instead of their becoming disasters they become occasions for triumph. To bring about this transformation we require God's wisdom. In prayer we may ask for the wisdom we need (James 1: 5).

We sometimes speak of prayer as asking as if we shouldn't. But any such sense of apology is unnecessary, and is perhaps a failure to grasp the extent of our Father's love for His children. Of course, prayer is much more than asking, but that doesn't diminish the fact that it has asking at its heart. When our Lord Jesus Christ spoke about our asking, seeking and knocking, He went on immediately to say, 'Which of you, if his son asks for bread, will give him a stone? Or if he asks for a fish, will give him a snake? If you, then, though you are evil, know how to give good gifts to your children, how much more will your Father in heaven give good gifts to those who ask him!' (Matthew 7: 9-11). 'Your Father in heaven' - that's the key. Born into God's family, we're His children. He's not just *like* a father to us, He *is* our Father. As young children live their lives in dependence upon their earthly father's resources, and by frequent asking, so we're to live our lives depending upon our heavenly Father's immeasurable resources, and by daily and frequent asking.

God's adoption of us into His family, through the Lord Jesus Christ, is the foundation of our prayer and our asking. United to His Son, God always hears us (cf John 11:41). He's never too busy, or too preoccupied to listen. A child has access to its father when such access may not be granted to anyone else. To assure us of this welcome, the Father and the Son have given us the Holy Spirit, who enables us to cry, 'Abba, Father'. 'Abba' derives originally from baby language. In the Aramaic language a baby learnt to say 'Abba' (Daddy) and 'Imma' (Mummy). But as time went on, the word widened in its meaning and was used in adult language for 'father' so that the childish character receded, and it acquired a more warm and familiar ring, such as we find in the words 'Dear Father!'

In the garden of Gethsemane, the Lord Jesus Himself began His prayer with the words 'Abba, Father' (Mark 14: 36). For first-century Jews, it was an entirely new expression to use in talking to God. It pinpoints the difference the Lord Jesus Christ brings to our relationship with God. Because we're sons and daughters, 'God sent the Spirit of his Son into our hearts, the Spirit who calls out, "Abba, Father"' (Galatians 4: 6).

As a human father, with four children, part and parcel of my particular relationship with them when they were younger was that they were always asking me for things. Our relationship, then and now, consists of much more than this, but there would be something seriously wrong if it didn't also include this. Human fathers - although they may not always admit it - enjoy providing for their children, for it's an essential part of fatherhood. Our heavenly Father tells us that He enjoys providing for us, and that we please Him by asking!

Asking takes many forms. It may be a straightforward cry for help (Psalm 34: 6; 39: 12) when we're in situations totally beyond our power to control. Sometimes it may be the simple declaration of need when we can't even see how we should ask God to supply it. When Mary took the initiative at the wedding in Cana of Galilee in going to Jesus and declaring, 'They have no more wine' (John 2: 3), she was doing what we very often have to do in prayer. We declare our need to God - not presuming to tell Him how He should choose to meet it - knowing that the honest declaration of our urgent need constitutes a request for help which He won't ignore.

A key factor in asking is knowing *how* we should ask and *for what* we should ask. Obviously we should aim at asking God for *good* things (Matthew 7: 11). He won't answer our prayers if we ask Him for things He knows will harm us - like a stone in place of bread, or a snake in place of a fish (Matthew 7: 9, 10). Where we can be specific in our requests, God is pleased because we then honour Him by our faith through looking for specific answers.

A number of questions immediately surface in our minds. How do we know what we should ask for? Should we pray for physical healing when we're ill? Should we pray for the gifts of the Spirit? How long should we go on asking God for the same things? In fact, why go on asking the Lord for something if we've asked once?

The Bible itself is our best guide as to the things which we should ask for. First, it tells us the things that are good and pleasing to God. Second, it is full of the prayers of others which are examples and patterns to follow. The Lord's Prayer - which we shall look at later - is an obvious example. The book of Psalms teems with prayers, and Paul's letters are liberally sprinkled with them. And, third, the Bible reveals God's Name, God's character. The test of much of our asking is the answer to the question, 'Is this request in accord with God's character?'

Physical healing - both for others and ourselves - is a

legitimate subject for prayer, as too are the gifts of the Spirit. But here, once more, the Bible - God's revealed will - must be our guide. Physical healing may be God's will in some cases, and not in others. Paul initially expected healing with regard to his 'thorn in the flesh' (2 Corinthians 12: 8) but God's answer was 'No'.

In the matter of spiritual gifts, the Scriptures must again be our guide. All the gifts are 'the work of one and the same Spirit, and he gives them to each man, just as he determines' (1 Corinthians 12: 11). So while it's appropriate to pray about them and to ask for a particular gift if we feel that's right, we must at the same time accept the guidance of the Scriptures that the gifts are given *as the Spirit determines* rather than as we may request.

We should go on asking for the same things - if we believe them to be God's will - until we either discover that He says 'No' or we have such an awareness of His peace about the particular matter that we know that to ask any more would be a lack of faith in Him. There are times when God wants us to persist in praying for something so that we assure ourselves of our own earnestness and keep ourselves available to become part of God's answer to our own prayers. I am thinking here of the conversion of close relatives and friends.

There are other areas of concern where to persist in praying about them indicates a lack of confidence in God rather than confidence in Him. The distinction between the two probably has something to do with whether or not I'm asking God for something which is for my own personal advantage, or something which I know God plainly wants for others. If I'm asking God for something for myself, which I know may or may not be His will, then to continue to ask Him for this same thing may well be inappropriate. Knowing He has heard my prayer, I may trust Him to do what's best. On the other hand, if I'm praying for the conversion of others, for those whom the Father has given to His Son as a fruit of Calvary, then I'm right to continue in my asking until I see God's answer, for in some mysterious way my praying, together with that of others, has a place in the unseen spiritual battle that goes on for men's souls. I seldom if ever in this life know what place my prayers may have, but I do know that when I pray I have the privilege of opening the resources of heaven to those for whom I pray.

Understandable yet a mystery

Earlier we likened prayer to the human pulse. It's a necessity. 'Without faith it is impossible to please God' (Hebrews 11:6), and prayer naturally expresses faith - it's faith's breath. Writing of Jerusalem's spiritual failure, the prophet Zephaniah declared, 'She does not trust in the Lord, she does not draw near to her God' (Zephaniah 3:2). Trusting in the Lord and drawing near to Him are one and the same.

We won't know all the answers to our questions about prayer until the time arrives when prayer will no longer be necessary! There's an essential mystery about it. It seems plain from history, however, that when God is about to work in some particular way He frequently lays a burden upon His people to pray for that very thing. Somehow or other, prayer is a necessary part of God's chosen way of doing things.

We can't overestimate the privilege of prayer. If we had unlimited access to our head of state, we would be regarded as not only fortunate but as influential, particularly if we had the ear of that person. How tremendous is our privilege of having access to the King of kings, and to 'have His ear'! The influence of prayer in the affairs of men and women worldwide is nothing less than the power of God.

A prayer

Father, first, I want to thank You for the privilege of calling You 'Abba, Father'. I remember with amazement the cost at which this right was obtained for me - the atoning sacrifice of Your Son upon the Cross. Please teach me to pray, and how to pray. Help me to learn to pray through praying. May prayer mean to me all that You intend it to mean for Your children. May it become as natural as breathing, and as satisfying to my soul as food and drink are to my body. For Your Son Jesus Christ's sake. Amen.

2

Prayer and the Christian Life

Christian living and prayer go hand in hand. All who live the Christian life successfully pray, and all who pray as God intends, do so as an expression of the new life God imparts through His Spirit as we put our trust in His Son Jesus Christ, and confess Him as Lord.

The fact that prayer is so automatic and essential a part of Christian experience doesn't mean that we don't have questions about prayer. There are many aspects of prayer that I don't understand. But the things I do know encourage me to pray because they are far greater than the things about which I'm uncertain.

Questions most of us ask

'How important is prayer?' *'Why pray at all?'* *'Can we change God's mind in prayer?'*

Exhaustive and definitive answers can't be provided to these questions. How, for example, do we measure importance? We may helpfully express the importance of prayer by a number of negatives. To neglect prayer is to neglect God. To fail to pray is to fail to enter into the majority of the blessings God wants to give. To be prayerless is to be powerless.

Positively, prayer is important because it's a vital expression of our personal relationship to God through Jesus Christ. It's our daily lifeline, and especially in times of trouble or difficulty. Not least it's important because it's commanded. The Lord Jesus told a parable to teach His disciples that 'they should always pray and not give up' (Luke 18: 1) and Paul urged the Thessalonians to 'Pray, continuously' (1 Thessalonians 5: 17).

'Can we change God's mind?' 'If God's plan is already worked out, how is prayer going to alter God's plan?'

Initially these questions appear reasonable, but they're really out of place because they're totally influenced by our human way of thinking and behaviour. We frequently change our minds because we feel we've made a mistake or arrived at a wrong decision, and we naturally want to rectify the situation where possible. At other times we feel that although we haven't perhaps made an entirely wrong decision, we can improve upon it. But God never makes mistakes, and He never decides upon a course of action only to discover later that it can be improved upon in some way. Balaam rebuked Balak, 'God is not a man... that he should change his mind. Does he speak and then not act? Does he promise and not fulfil?' (Numbers 23: 19).

God may *appear* to change His mind in answer to our prayers, whereas in fact, He knows all the time what He intends to do. We find a good example in Abraham's interceding for Sodom (Genesis 18: 16-33). The incident significantly records God asking, 'Shall I hide from Abraham what I am about to do?' (17). God knew from the beginning His ultimate action, but because Abraham was God's friend he was going to be let into God's secret and have a share in the implementing of God's will. Made aware of God's impending judgment on Sodom, Abraham was stirred to pray for Sodom - and that was precisely what God wanted him to do! Abraham's intercession didn't and couldn't alter the inevitability of God's righteous judgment upon Sodom, but it did bring to Abraham - and also to us as we read the historical record - an understanding of God's compassion for even as few as ten righteous people if they could be found in such an appallingly sinful city.

What place do our prayers have in God's plans and purposes?

An explanation that helps, at least in part, is that the broad outlines of God's plans are already established from eternity. So, for example, God is going to 'bring all things in heaven and on earth together under one head, even Christ' (Ephesians 1: 10). That's plainly an unalterable purpose of God. Now my prayers would never want to be directed towards any alteration of such a glorious intention. Rather they're guided by such a purpose. God - who made man in His own image, and who renews that image in me through my union with the Lord Jesus - desires my involvement in His great purposes, and one of the means by which that is achieved - although mysterious and beyond my comprehension - is my praying in harmony with what He has shown to be His plan and purpose.

Furthermore, God's plans and purposes are always good, and I may be absolutely sure that men and women are never shut out of them without just cause. Because I know that God is good - all that He as God ought to be - my desire in prayer should never be to change His mind. Rather it will be my mind that needs changing to His, so that I ask for the good things, and the best.

God answers prayer

The basic answer to all our questions as to the importance and place of prayer in the Christian life is the simple yet profound truth that God answers prayer - our requests are heard (Matthew 7: 7-11; 18: 19; John 16: 23, 24, 26; James 1: 5; 1 John 3: 21, 22; 5: 14f). There wouldn't be any point whatsoever in prayer if we didn't have this assurance. Prayer is the means God Himself has appointed so that we may obtain fresh experiences of His power. There are situations in life in which He says to us, 'This kind can come out only by prayer' (Mark 9: 29).

Prayer is the appointed means of obtaining blessing. It's a necessary part of our cooperation with God, especially when we need some special deliverance (2 Corinthians 1: 10, 11).

Our Lord Jesus Christ went to great pains in His teaching to underline God's essential provision of prayer for the living of the Christian life. 'Ask,' He urged, 'and *it will be given to you* ; seek *and you will find* ; knock *and the door will be opened to you* (Matthew 7: 7). He then amplified it, 'For everyone who asks receives; he who seeks finds; and to him who knocks, the door will be opened' (Matthew 7: 8). 'If you remain in me', He said, 'and my words remain in you, ask whatever you wish, and it will be given you' (John 15: 7).

The confidence that God delights to answer our prayers is one of the greatest possible incentives to pray. God our Father doesn't hear our prayers grudgingly, but willingly. He Himself prompts our requests because it's His purpose to answer them! He answers our prayers not so much as a favour but as a pleasure. God our Father loves us more than any earthly father loves a son or daughter, and He won't allow any request to pass unnoticed or unanswered. I, as a fallible human father, find immense pleasure in meeting the requests of my children. If it's a present I know they want, then I'll spend hours searching for just the right one. If it's something I'm to do or make for them, no effort is too much trouble to provide the best. God's Fatherhood is not modelled on mine - rather mine is modelled, all too inadequately, on His, and He is the perfect Father!

An identifying mark

Prayer is part of the evidence that a man or woman has become a Christian, that the new birth has taken place. The first recorded activity of the converted Saul was that he prayed (Acts 9: 11), an activity entirely in accord with the New Testament teaching that all who belong to Christ possess the Holy Spirit (Romans 8: 9) and by His help cry '*Abba*, Father' (Romans 8: 15). When we are 'in Christ' prayer should be an entirely natural process - like eating and breathing. As a Puritan writer put it, 'God has none of His children born dumb'. Or as James Montgomery expresses it in one of his hymns, 'Prayer is the Christian's vital breath, the Christian's native air'. Such statements aren't to be passed over lightly. A prayerless spirit isn't synonymous with the possession of the Holy Spirit. When prayer remains absent, the probability is that the Spirit of Christ, who indwells every believer, is either not present or, if present, is grieved or quenched through disobedience.

The complement of obedience

Prayer is the natural complement to the obedience that's implicit in Christian discipleship. If we have to choose one word to express the key to Christian experience, then obedience is that key word. 'If you love me, you will obey what I command', the Lord Jesus explained (John 14: 15). Obedience is the 'open sesame' to the most profound and deep fellowship with God. 'If anyone loves me', Jesus promises, 'he will obey my teaching. My Father will love him, *and we will come to him and make our home with him*'(John 14: 23).

Prayer is an essential part of our obedience to Jesus' teaching (e.g. Luke 18: 1) and also to the Holy Spirit's promptings and encouragements. Prayer is an invaluable means by which our soul and mind may be impressed by convictions as to the right action God is commanding. Furthermore, prayer is the secret of the strength we need to obey God when obedience itself is difficult.

Obedience and prayer can't be separated. Obedience - our desire for it, as well as its implementation - requires prayer. Prayer has as one of its proper assumptions our desire to obey God. John spelt out this truth in his first letter: 'Dear friends, if our hearts do not condemn us, we have confidence before God and receive from him anything we ask, because we obey his commands and do what pleases him' (1 John 3: 21,22). The more obedient we are to God, the more confident we're likely to find ourselves in prayer - not because our obedience in some way merits God's answers, but because the Holy Spirit delights to give assurance to the obedient that their prayers are heard. None had greater confidence in the Father's willingness to answer prayer than our Lord Jesus Christ Himself. None has matched - nor will ever match - His obedience to the Father, for the words 'I have come to do your will, O God' sum up His earthly life (Hebrews 10: 7). The Christian life is above everything else a life of obedience. That obedience expresses itself in prayer, and is itself furthered and strengthened by prayer.

A way of escape

Temptations and trials are an inevitable part of daily life, and also of the Christian life. To escape them we would have to escape out of the world altogether. They seldom, if ever, become less of a problem, and they turn up in a variety of permutations. Prayer is the Christian's principal way of escape in times of temptation and trial. It's significant that the request for wisdom from God - a request the Bible encourages us to make - occurs in the context of the trials and temptations of life (James 1: 2-5). Deliverance is always God's will in times of temptation, and strength to endure and persevere is God's consistent purpose for us in trials.

Deliverance comes through prayer - as David testified, 'This poor man called, and the Lord heard him; he saved him out of all his troubles' (Psalm 34: 6). As we call upon God, He may sometimes provide a literal way of escape through an amazing intervention or change of circumstance. But more often than not He provides us with an inner strengthening which enables us to 'stand up under it' (1 Corinthians 10: 13). Gethsemane constituted both a trial and temptation to our Lord Jesus: a trial the Father permitted, and a temptation Satan threw at the Lord Jesus to try to divert Him from His obedience to the pathway of the Cross. But as our Lord prayed, He discovered the promised way of escape (1 Corinthians 10: 13). It wasn't a change of direction or circumstance, but it was an influx of strength: 'An angel from heaven appeared to him and strengthened him' (Luke 22: 43).

While many habits and sinful features of our pre-conversion life may die immediately upon our conversion, others may not. William Thomas entered into God's salvation through the witness of a church in Aberavon in Wales. The change in him was remarkable, but he didn't share with his fellow believers at the beginning the struggle he experienced with his lifelong use of bad language. It wasn't so much that he meant it, but he couldn't speak without interspersing all he said with oaths and blasphemies. It threw him into abject misery. But deliverance came about through prayer:

'... he was getting up one morning and gathering his clothes together to get dressed. But there were no socks among his clothes. He went to the bedroom door and shouted to his wife "I can't find my --- socks! Where are the --- things?" As he heard himself speak and realised what he had just said, a great horror possessed him and he fell back on the bed in a paroxysm of despair, and cried aloud, "O Lord, cleanse my tongue. O Lord, I can't ask for a pair of socks without swearing, please have mercy on me and give me a clean tongue." And as he lay there, and as he got up from that bed, he knew that God had done for him what he could not do for himself. His prayer, his cry of agony was heard and answered, and it was his testimony that from that moment to the end of his days no swear word, or foul or blasphemous word, ever again passed his lips' (Ian H Murray: *D M Lloyd-Jones. The First Forty Years 1899-1939* , p.244).

Prayer is always an important part of God's provision for us in the time of temptation, and sometimes it's the whole answer. When we're tried and tested, to be able to pray is frequently the safety valve we need, which mercifully saves us from becoming a problem and a burden to others.

The secret weapon

God intends that no Christian should find the Christian life too demanding or impossible. Prayer is part of God's equipping of us to be effective in our life and service. In 2 Timothy 2: 2-6 Paul gives three pictures of a Christian - a soldier, an athlete and a farmer. The soldier must be prepared for hardship - *prayer* brings strength to endure hardship. The athlete must be willing for severe self-discipline - *prayer* offers a pathway to self-discipline. The farmer must be content to work hard in all weathers, and to persist in following the divine pattern of sowing in order to gain a harvest - *prayer* renews our strength to work hard and to be confident of God's promised harvest. All the strength we need for successful obedience to the Lord Jesus is available - and the way to receive is to pray for what we require. A Christian who doesn't pray is like a fish out of water gasping for breath. He's like a man living as a down-and-out when he has the opportunity of living as the wealthiest person of whom he can think.

Prayer constitutes the Christian's secret weapon- secret in the sense that the world neither sees it being exercised very often nor believes in it. It's secret in that it can be exercised without anyone - except God and the person praying - being aware of it. The book of Daniel illustrates the powerful use to which Daniel and his three friends, Shadrach, Meshach and Abednego put this secret weapon. The Babylonians couldn't understand why these young men showed such promise and came to such prominence, but we have their secret when we discover them to be men who exercised their privilege of prayer. Nebuchadnezzar was amazed at Daniel's ability to interpret his dreams, but Daniel's secret was that he had urged his three friends 'to plead for mercy from the God of heaven concerning this mystery' (Daniel 2: 18). When Daniel's life was put under scrutiny by his jealous opponents, the only thing they could find 'wrong' with him was that 'three times a day he got down on his knees and prayed...' (Daniel 6: 10). Prayer achieved more in the affairs of Babylon than its inhabitants ever knew.

The climax of Paul's description of the armour God provides for the Christian life is the addition of two attacking weapons, the Scriptures and prayer: 'Take... the sword of the Spirit, which is the word of God,' he urges, 'And pray in the Spirit on all occasions with all kinds of prayers and requests' (Ephesians 6: 17, 18).

All attacks upon our spiritual well-being become weak before prayer's power. One night George Whitefield, the eighteenth-century evangelist, found himself spiritually out of sorts. He wrote in his diary, 'Was afterwards a little inclined to heaviness, but drove it off by a long intercession. *Prayer is an antidote against every evil.*'

One of the wonders of prayer is that it can be used as a secret weapon to accomplish changes that would be completely impossible otherwise. Charles Spurgeon related to a group of ministers the story of a church in New England which appointed a young man by the name of Stoddard to be its minister, only to find that he wasn't a real Christian. Instead of finding fault and quarrelling with him, the church was called together to pray. On that particular Sunday night, when his day's work was over, the young minister saw the people flocking to the church.

Surprised at their going in such numbers to a service at which he wasn't himself to preside, he asked someone, 'Why are they meeting?' In all innocence, not recognising the questioner, the person replied, 'They are coming together to pray that their minister may be converted.' The young minister went home, shut his door behind him, and prayed for himself and sought eternal life. Before the church prayer meeting ended, he was converted, and went down to the meeting to share the good news! There are innumerable battles and crises which find their answer uniquely in prayer. John Eliot (1604-90), who translated the Bible into the 'Moheecan' language, wrote at the end of his Indian grammar these words, 'Prayer and pains, through faith in Jesus Christ, will do anything.'

Prayer both partners and complements our use of the Bible. The Holy Spirit is intimately involved with both. He provides the Word of God, which is His sword - it results from His inspiration - and He prompts and assists prayer. The wise use of the Bible and the effective exercise of prayer are really two sides of the same coin. By means of the Bible God speaks to me; and by means of prayer I speak to God. Now that's an oversimplification but it's a basic truth to grasp. It's an oversimplification because by means of the Bible's instruction and guidance I learn to talk to God. Furthermore, in prayer God so often speaks to me. As I wait before Him in silence, or quietly meditate on His Word, His Spirit educates my conscience, and often convinces and convicts it. Through the Scriptures God guides me as to how I may win the spiritual battle of which prayer is such a vital part.

Aggressive prayer, based on God's Word, is invincible: 'The weapons we fight with are not the weapons of the world. On the contrary, they have divine power to demolish strongholds' (2 Corinthians 10: 4).

As with all weapons and tools, we learn to use them by practice, and we learn to pray by praying. 'Pray often,' John

Bunyan said, 'prayer is a shield to the soul, a sacrifice to God and a scourge of Satan.' We won't learn to swim by reading a book about swimming unless at the same time we're willing to enter the water. And so it is with prayer.

Maintaining our submission to God's will

Prayer is a key to our maintaining our proper submission to God's will. Christian obedience isn't achieved overnight - it's not immediate. In fact, it's a continuous daily process. The various experiences of life - such as bereavement, marriage, birth, promotion, retirement, and old age - involve constant adjustments to our way of life, our attitudes and our conduct to ensure that our obedience remains alive and active. In prayer we're able to share these experiences - and every other - with our heavenly Father and recognise the path of obedience to which He calls us. As fallen creatures it's natural to be inclined to think that we know best, but in prayer we humble ourselves before God, acknowledging that He alone is the One who knows best. While God resists the proud, He freely gives grace to the humble (James 4: 6; 1 Peter 5: 5).

Sometimes a battle takes place when we try to submit our will to God. Although we know, without doubt, that His will is 'good, pleasing and perfect' (Romans 12: 2), that assurance doesn't mean that submission to it is achieved without difficulty. Our initial perspective or attitude may be wrong. We may not be seeing God's mercy to us in the Lord Jesus as clearly as we ought (Romans 12: 1), and if that's the case we'll fail to respond properly. We may be overinfluenced by the patterns and values of this passing world. Our mind may be insufficiently renewed after the pattern of Christ's example. We may be thinking much too highly of ourselves.

Prayer has as one of its principal functions the submission of our will to God's. Prayer enables us to tell God that we want what He wants. That doesn't mean that we may not ask for whatever is uppermost in our desires, but we must be willing, at the same time, for our Father to say 'No'. We may sometimes question God about His will - as Moses did (Exodus 5: 22) - but basic to our questioning is that we still submit to Him if He doesn't choose to answer our questions. In prayer we remember that God's knowledge is superior to ours: He knows best, therefore, how to meet our needs (Psalm 139: 1-6). In prayer we endeavour to make our will coincide with God's (Romans 1: 10).

In their book *Mission to the Headhunters*, Frank and Marie Drown relate the following story of a missionary in Equador who was deeply moved as he found an Indian woman, belonging to what would be regarded as a 'primitive' tribe, kneeling in prayer. He knelt in the dirt beside her and prayed with her. 'An old woman, she was lifting her heart in praise to the Lord who had saved her, and in petition for His help and protection over her son. At this time he had gone on a long trip through the jungle to visit relatives and she was afraid for his safety.' And this was her prayer: '"But if my son should die on the trail from a bite of a snake, which is what I always fear," she said, "I will love and trust Thee, knowing I will see Mayapruwa again in Heaven."'

Each time we pray, our souls should be brought into a new submission to God's will. That's by no means easy in many critical situations. Our Lord Jesus Christ was deeply distressed as He contemplated in Gethsemane what He knew to be the Father's will for Him - the Cross. His soul was overwhelmed with sorrow to the point of death. He poured out His soul to the Father. He asked that the cup might be removed from Him but with one proviso: 'Yet not what I will, but what you will' (Mark 14: 36). Three times He prayed the same prayer.

Like our Saviour, we may be compelled to pray the same prayer several times before we're sure that we're in a position of genuine submission to God. We shouldn't hesitate to pray for the same thing time and again if we feel that our wills aren't entirely submitted to God in the way we know they should be. Our hearts and souls will find themselves searched as we honestly ask ourselves, 'Do I really want what God wants?' But peace becomes ours when we arrive at the position where we can honestly say 'Yes' to God's will. In the period between asking such a question and then finding God's peace in submission to His will there may be what can only be described as 'wrestling in prayer'. We may have to wrestle with conflicting emotions, with a mixture of motives, and with our secret fears as to what God's will may involve if we fully submit to it. It may be only after intense struggle that we're able to identify our will with God's - and sometimes it may be with tears. But if at the end we can say, with David, 'I stay close to you' (Psalm 63: 8), then it will be worth it all.

Prayer is a significant exercise of the shield of faith (Ephesians 6: 16, 18). The great enemy of our souls, Satan, always tries to make us magnify the difficulties and hardships of God's will. He constantly tries to make us read the worst possible implications into what may appear to be God's purpose for us. In prayer we lift up the shield of faith against Satan, and affirm that God's will is *always* good.

Grace and peace day by day

Prayer is the secret of our daily enjoyment of God's grace and peace. All Paul's letters begin with a prayer - a prayer which includes as its most vital element the request for grace and peace to be the enjoyment of his readers (Romans 1: 7; 1 Corinthians 1: 3; 2 Corinthians 1: 2 etc). This prayerful greeting may be so familiar that we pass over its significance.

Grace is God dealing with us with an amazing kindness we could never merit or deserve. While our new birth means that we hate sin as we never did before, and we daily strive to turn from it, living closer to God we appreciate more than ever before the extent of our sinfulness. A day doesn't pass without our being made aware in some way of our falling short of God's will and commandments. Our experience of God's grace in forgiveness, therefore, is a daily necessity (1 John 1: 9). In addition, times of difficulty highlight our requirement of grace to 'help us in our time of need' and we obtain that grace at the throne of grace (Hebrews 4: 16). Wonderfully, God 'gives us more grace' in response to prayer(James4:5,6, 8).

Grace's companion is peace. When my experience of God's grace is fresh, I'm in a position to share my life with Him completely so as to discover anew His peace. In Numbers 6: 24ff, peace sums up all the other blessings God gives, and it's closely associated with His presence with us. Peace is equivalent to sharing all the blessing of salvation. I have peace when I know that God is *for me,* and *for me* in what may be a difficult situation. In prayer I may tell God *everything,* and as I do so I may have the confidence that He takes care of everything. 'Do not be anxious about anything,' Paul urged, 'but in everything, by prayer and petition, with thanksgiving, present your requests to God. And the peace of God which transcends all understanding, will guard your hearts and your minds in Christ Jesus' (Philippians 4: 6, 7).

We mustn't overlook how practical and down-to-earth God's peace is. When Dr and Mrs Martyn Lloyd-Jones served the Church at Sandfields in Wales, their home was very close to the sea. The south-west gales blowing in from the sea could be terrifying, especially as disasters had occurred there in the past. Mrs Lloyd-Jones tells her own story:

'One night when Martyn was away, and I was alone with the baby, there was an exceptionally severe gale blowing in from the sea, and I lay, beside myself with fear, tossing feverishly in my bed, full of terror and panic - if the tide came up Victoria Road, could I escape with the baby? Get out of the window? On the roof? etc. At last, in sheer helpless despair, I got out of my bed and on to my knees, and I prayed: "Lord, if it is all true, if You are really there and will answer my prayer, *please* give me peace and take all my fear away". As I spoke, it all went away, my heart was flooded with perfect peace, and I never had any more fear of gales and tides. I was completely delivered and asleep in two minutes' (Iain Murray:*D M Lloyd Jones The First Forty Years 1899-1939*, p 239).

Prayer tranquillises the most perturbed mind. Irritated, overcome by trouble, the storm calms and the irritation is seen in perspective as we pray. Prayer enables us to obtain good from our trials, and it turns our sorrows into joys (see Psalm 30: 8-12). Henry Martyn, a lonely young missionary in India, keenly aware that he wasn't going to see again the young woman in England whom he loved, wrote, 'I received a letter from Lydia today which renewed my pain, though it contained nothing but what I expected. Prayer was my only relief and I found peace by casting my care on God.'

Faith and works

The Christian life demands a life of faith *and* works. Faith and works aren't in conflict; rather they're meant to be in perfect harmony in the Christian's life. 'Without faith it is impossible to please God, because anyone who comes to him must believe that he exists and that he rewards those who earnestly seek him' (Hebrews 11: 6). True prayer is the natural exercise of faith. But the proof that it's true faith will be seen in the works that accompany the prayer.

Prayer and action go hand in hand - they are inseparable twins. When I pray aright, I then act in the light of my praying - this is true both for me as an individual and in my praying with other believers. Basic to this whole matter of the relationship between prayer and action is the importance of being specific in our prayers, where possible. Unspecific prayers may easily lead to unspecific action - and most frequently no action - whereas specific prayers prompt specific anticipation and action.

Abraham's servant had the difficult task of finding a suitable bride for his master Abraham's son, Isaac. He arrived in the neighbourhood to which Abraham had directed him, and he prayed, 'O Lord, God of my master Abraham, give me success today, and show kindness to my master Abraham. See, I am standing beside this spring, and the daughters of the townspeople are coming out to draw water. May it be that when I say to a girl, "Please let down your jar that I may have a drink," and she says, "Drink and I'll water your camels too" - let her be the one you have chosen for your servant Isaac. By this I will know that you have shown kindness to my master.' That was certainly specific prayer! The Genesis record continues: 'Before he had finished praying, Rebekah came out with her jar on her shoulder. She was the daughter of Bethuel son of Milcah, who was the wife of Abraham's brother...' (Genesis 24: 12-15). 'The servant hurried to meet her and said, "Please give me a little water from your jar"' (Genesis 24: 17), and his prayer was answered. But it had required his action to accompany it.

The same principle applies in corporate prayer. The early believers in Jerusalem were instructed by the Jewish authorities not to preach any more in the Name of Jesus. They met together to pray, and cried, 'Lord, consider their threats and enable your servants to speak your word with great boldness' (Acts 4: 29). 'After they prayed, the place where they were meeting was shaken. And they were all filled with the Holy Spirit and spoke the word of

God boldly' (Acts 4: 31). Amazing progress took place because these early Christians prayed with the readiness to act in the light of their prayers - they held themselves available to be part of God's answer to their prayers. Paul wrote of 'the obedience of faith' or 'the obedience that comes from faith' (Romans 1: 5), and prayer linked with action and issuing in action, is an essential part of that obedience. Faith without works is dead, and so too is prayer.

A prayer

Father, may my praying show me to be one of Your children; and through prayer may I find strength to obey and keep Your commandments. When I'm tested or tempted, may I never miss the way of escape that prayer affords. Help me to use prayer as a weapon to pull down Satan's strongholds. I want to submit myself now to Your good and perfect will. May my life overflow with Your grace and peace to the glory of Your Name. May my prayers prove themselves to be prayers of faith as I back them up by action. For Jesus' sake. Amen.

3
Prayer's Potential

'What's the potential of nuclear energy?' The correct answer must be something like, 'It's tremendous, probably beyond the immediate grasp of the human mind, and it has yet to be fully realised.' The same kind of thing - only more so - must be said of prayer. Its potential is synonymous with the power of God and, like that power, it's beyond our minds to grasp its immensity. No Christian has yet exhausted its capabilities.

The testimony of the ages

In every period of history believers have affirmed prayer's glorious potential, summed up in David's simple testimony: 'This poor man called, and the Lord heard him; he saved him out of all his troubles' (Psalm 34: 6). David's experience has been repeated - and is repeated daily - thousands of times. We don't have to be Christians for long before we can look back and recognise many answers to our prayers.

Some sceptics might suggest that what we claim to be 'answers' have been 'coincidences'. But we can answer, with complete honesty, that if we only had a few answers they might be considered coincidences but God *continually* answers our prayers. Some answers are too personal to share with others. But as certainly as we know we're alive, we know God answers our prayers.

In the Name of Jesus

Prayer's potential is that it's 'in the Name of Jesus'. It's our habit to end our prayers with phrases like 'In Jesus' Name' or 'For Jesus Christ's sake'. Behind this right conclusion to our prayers, there's Jesus' own teaching that prayer should be in His Name. In John 14-16 the phrase 'in my name' occurs seven times (14: 13, 14, 26; 15: 16; 16: 23, 24, 26) and John 15: 16 is typical: 'the Father will give you whatever you ask in my name'. The words 'in the Name of Jesus' aren't a kind of magical formula we attach to our prayers to guarantee their success. We don't simply ask for whatever we want and then by adding the words 'in Jesus' Name' expect our requests to be auto- matically answered - perhaps treating Jesus' Name as the code to be employed as we might key in a number in a bank cash dispenser before we press the button for the money we request.

Faith in His Name

Prayer in Jesus' Name is prayer which has as its foun- dation faith in His Name. His Name - *Jesus* - means Sav- iour. We may make our requests in His Name because He is our Mediator: 'For there is one God and one mediator between God and men, the man Christ Jesus, who gave himself as a ransom for all men' (1 Timothy 2: 5, 6).

It's quite impossible for us to approach God in our own name, by virtue of our own merits, and be accepted. He's holy, and we are unclean and completely unaccept- able to Him by reason of our sin, but our Saviour's worthiness provides us with complete acceptance with God. We come before God trusting in Jesus' sacrifice, and pleading the merits of His atoning blood. Our ground of acceptance is His merit, not ours, and we offer our prayers to God in the Name of the One whom He has appointed to be our Mediator. To pray in Jesus' Name is to be trusting the Lord Jesus' saving work as the sole ground of our access to God. It is to know that our approach to God's throne of grace is through His own grace given us in His Son. It's faith in Jesus' Name which the Father looks for in particular.

Practical Prayer

Harmony with His Name

A 'name' doesn't mean much in our culture but in the ancient world it stood for the whole personality. A man's name is what he *is* . The Lord Jesus deliberately revealed the Father's Name - He showed us the Father. To pray in Jesus' Name is to pray in harmony with the revelation He has given of the Father; it is to ask for those things which are in complete keeping with Jesus' character as we know it.

Suppose we want to pray for a widow who's been bereaved once more, this time of one of her children; how are we to pray in Jesus' Name for her? I would suggest that the revelation of God's love which Jesus gave in His command at the time of His crucifixion is our guide. John tells us, 'When Jesus saw his mother there, and the disciple whom he loved standing near by, he said to his mother, "Dear woman, here is your son," and to the disciple, "Here is your mother". From that time on, this disciple took her into his home' (John 19: 26, 27). Praying in Jesus' Name for a widow bereaved of her child may mean praying that she'll be comforted by the care and love of someone who feels a personal sense of responsibility for her.

Suppose we're praying for the millions who haven't yet heard the good news of Jesus and His kingdom. Matthew tells us that when Jesus 'saw the crowds, he had compassion on them, because they were harassed and helpless, like sheep without a shepherd. Then he said to his disciples, "The harvest is plentiful but the workers are few. Ask the Lord of the harvest, therefore, to send out workers into his harvest field"' (Matthew 9: 36-38). To pray in Jesus' Name - to pray in harmony with the revelation He gives of God and of His will - is to pray for compassion, and for the ability to see people's spiritual need as that of sheep needing a Shepherd. To pray in Jesus' Name then is to pray that workers will be sent out,

41

making sure that we ourselves are also available as part of God's answer to our prayers, if that's what He wants. Such prayer is in Jesus' Name because it's in total harmony with the revelation He has given both by word and by example.

Reflecting our union with Him

God's amazing goodness to us in Jesus Christ finds innumerable expressions. One of the most glorious and exciting New Testament truths is that He unites us to Jesus Christ - the favourite New Testament description of a Christian is someone who is 'in Christ'. United to Jesus Christ, we share all the benefits of His death, resurrection and ascension. Rather like a woman who upon marriage takes her husband's name and shares all his resources, so we take Jesus' Name and we share all His resources. A loving wife is glad to bear her husband's name; and in her use of his name and his resources, she wants to please him.

Prayer in Jesus' Name is prayer that reflects our union with Him. It's not a presumption on our part to declare that all His resources are ours: He tells us that they are! We may think of God's promises like cheques. They require two signatures: Jesus Christ's and ours. The Lord Jesus has already signed the cheques because of our union with Him. We only have to present them at Heaven's Bank!

The honour of Jesus' Name

Prayer in Jesus' Name is prayer that has His honour in view. To act in someone's name is to act as that person's representative. To pray in Jesus' Name is to see ourselves as His representatives and to ask the Father for the benefits we know will honour His Son and forward His kingdom. Prayer in Jesus' Name is prayer that seeks the glory of His Name. Acts 4 provides an instructive example. Peter and John had preached in Jesus' Name. 'Salvation,' they declared, 'is found in no-one else, for there is no other name under heaven given to men by which we must be saved' (Acts 4: 12). They were ordered 'to speak no longer to anyone in this name' (17). What were they to do? Their Lord, whose representatives they were, had instructed them to preach the good news to every creature. Their solution was to raise their voices together in prayer to God. They recalled before God what the Jewish people had done to His 'holy servant Jesus' (27) and they prayed, 'Lord, consider their threats and enable your servants to speak your word with great boldness. Stretch out your hand to heal and perform miraculous signs and wonders through the name of your holy servant Jesus' (29, 30). And He did! Their conspicuous motive was the honour and glory of Jesus' Name.

When we pray in Jesus' Name we genuinely want only what He wants. The Prayer Book Collect for the Tenth Sunday after Trinity puts it well, quaint as the language now seems, 'Let thy merciful ears, O Lord, be open to the prayers of thy humble servants; and that they may obtain their petitions make them to ask such things as shall please thee; through Jesus Christ our Lord. *Amen.*' Prayer in Jesus' Name is prayer that is consistent with what we know He would have us ask.

The authority of Jesus' Name

Jesus' Name is the name of greatest authority because He is the unique Son of God, in whom the Father delights. There is none whom the Father loves more than the Son. The essence of the eternal happiness of the Godhead is the Father's delight in the Son, and the Son's delight in the Father. One of the ways in which the Father honours His Son is the authority He gives to His Son's Name.

Furthermore, in the plan of salvation God's deliberate purpose has been that in everything His Son should have first place. The Lord Jesus is 'the head of the body, the church', Paul writes, 'he is the beginning and the firstborn from among the dead, so that in everything he might have the supremacy. For God was pleased to have all his fulness dwell in him, and through him to reconcile to himself all things, whether things on earth or things in heaven, by making peace through his blood, shed on the cross' (Colossians 1: 18-20). Or, as Paul wrote to the Philippians, probably quoting an early Christian song, 'Therefore God exalted him to the highest place and gave him the name that is above every name, that at the name of Jesus every knee should bow, in heaven and on earth and under the earth, and every tongue confess that Jesus Christ is Lord, to the glory of God the Father' (Philippians 2: 9-11).

The essential potential of prayer is the authority of Jesus' Name. As John Newton expressed it:

'Thou art coming to a King,
Large petitions with thee bring;
For His grace and power are such,
None can ever ask too much.'

Prayer's potential is power

'Wisdom is better than weapons of war' (Ecclesiastes 9: 18) and we are never wiser and closer to power than when we pray in Jesus' Name. James affirms that 'The prayer of a righteous man is powerful and effective' (James 5: 16). By a righteous man he means first and foremost a man who is in a right relationship with God - a reconciled man. But he means more than that; he has in view the reconciled man who shows that he is such by his desires and strivings to live rightly. He illustrates the power and effectiveness of prayer by means of Elijah - a

44

man just like us - who 'prayed earnestly that it would not rain, and it did not rain on the land for three and a half years. Again he prayed, and the heavens gave rain, and the earth produced its crops' (James 5: 17, 18). God's answer to Elijah's prayers gave proof that Elijah was God's servant (1 Kings 18: 36), and this seems to have been the case too with regard to the prayers of Paul and Silas in the prison at Philippi (Acts 16: 25, 26).

Prayer - and the answers God gives - mark us out as God's servants in the world. Prayer also makes us the kind of Christians Satan has learned to fear. When we pray we're a threat to the stability of Satan's government in the lives of men and women. He can't be sure of himself, for by prayer we gain power and authority to restrict him, and in some situations even to bind him. By prayer we declare war on Satan, with the rightful confidence that our power - God's power - is more than sufficient to overcome him.

The history of God's people provides countless illustrations of prayer's power. At the beginning of this century the Boxer uprising took place in China. Many missionaries found their lives in jeopardy. The Rev. and Mrs Archibald Glover, their two small children, and a fellow missionary, Miss Gates, made an amazing journey to the coast from inland China, with repeated hair's-breadth escapes from death. On one occasion they were put in prison for the night, and Miss Gates heard one of their gaolers give the instruction to kill them that night by poisoning them with opium, stupifying them first of all by burning a narcotic in their cell. 'Without giving the gaolers the slightest intimation that we had understood what had passed, we made our prayer to God,' Mr Glover writes, 'and set a watch against them.' The gaoler went about his task, and the atmosphere nearly drove the victims into unconsciousness, but the narcotic didn't succeed. In the morning the gaolers had great difficulty deciding what to say to their boss. The missionaries heard them announce their decision. They would say: 'These people have been praying to God, and we could do nothing against their prayers'.

A Christian newspaper called *Revival*, later known as *The Christian* reported on D L Moody's work in America. A bedridden girl, Marianne Adlard, in London read the story, and she began to pray, 'O Lord, send this man to our church'. She had no means of reaching him or communicating with him. Moody had visited Britain once before, and now five years later he started again for a short trip without any intention of doing any evangelistic work here. But who should meet him but the pastor of this young girl's church, and he asked Moody to preach for him. Now that in itself was remarkable, but it wasn't all. At the service at which he preached in this girl's church, Moody asked those who would decide for Christ that night to rise. Hundreds did so! He was surprised, and imagined that his request had been misunderstood. He repeated it more clearly, and the response was the same. Meetings were continued throughout the following ten days, and four hundred members were taken into the church as a result! To quote Moody, 'I wanted to know what this meant. I began making enquiries, and never rested until I found a bedridden girl praying that God would bring me to that church. He had heard her, and brought me over four thousand miles of land and sea in answer to her request.'

Prayer in the Name of Jesus is powerfully able to move the heart of the Father. True prayer in Jesus' Name is true power. Fresh proofs occur every day.

Deliverance

Deliverance is a principal evidence of prayer's potential. The deliverance may be physical - where such is God's will - or it may be spiritual, a benefit which is invariably God's will for His people. David's testimony -

already referred to - 'This poor man called, and the Lord heard him; he saved him out of all his troubles' (Psalm 34: 6), is not only typical of the Old Testament psalms but it's typical of Christian experience. Writing from prison, with his future uncertain, Paul wrote to his Philippian friends, 'Yes, and I will continue to rejoice, for I know that through your prayers and the help given by the Spirit of Jesus Christ, what has happened to me will turn out for my deliverance' (Philippians 1: 18, 19).

Prayer's potential is that it brings God into human situations so that they must get better, and can only change for the good. Prayer brings help when there appears, to the human eye, to be no possibility of help. David recalled a personal emergency when he wrote, 'Praise be to the Lord, for he showed his wonderful love to me when I was in a besieged city. In my alarm I said, "I am cut off from your sight!" Yet you heard my cry for mercy when I called to you for help' (Psalm 31: 21, 22). When circumstances dictate giving in, or abandoning ourselves to despair, prayer brings deliverance and even joy without the immediate circumstances changing. If we think it through we have to conclude that a praying man or woman can never be miserable - or, at least, can't remain miserable!

No Limit

Prayer's potential is such that no limit can be put on it. God can do 'immeasurably more than all we ask or imagine, according to his power that is at work within us' (Ephesians 3: 20). 'More things are wrought by prayer than this world dreams of.' Prayer's potential is that, amazingly, there are no small things with God. His involvement in our lives is complete. We are so important to Him that everything that touches and concerns us, touches and concerns Him. We're able to pray about everything, as often and as many times as we need.

A Question

If prayer's potential is so great, why is it that we don't prove its full potential as we ought? First, we may be lacking in faith; and secondly, we may not take prayer seriously.

Prayer's potential requires faith in order to be realised. As our faith is, so are our prayers. But that raises the question, 'Is *complete* faith absolutely critical to the answer?' Happily, the answer is 'No'. The Lord Jesus spoke of the possibility of having 'faith as small as a mustard seed' and yet of its being effective (Matthew 17: 20). It would seem plain from Acts 12 that when the believers prayed for Peter's deliverance from prison they didn't expect him to be knocking on the door that night as a free man! (Acts 12: 14, 15). Nevertheless the Christians showed their faith by gathering together in order to pray.

We all know the reality of doubts. There's a difference between praying with *doubt* and praying with *doubts*. If someone doubts the value of prayer, he's bound to pray in vain. That's quite different from coming to God in prayer, convinced that He answers prayer, but perhaps having doubts as to the validity of what we ask, or finding Satan trying to sow doubts in our minds as to either God's power or God's willingness to help us. Like the man in the Gospels, we may cry then with confidence to our Father, in Jesus' Name, 'I do believe; help me overcome my unbelief!' (Mark 9: 24). The right procedure with doubts is neither to hide them nor to pretend they don't exist but to bring them out into the open in God's presence, so that He may resolve them. In His light, we see light. Once we look into His face, we soon remember He's our Father, that His resources are limitless, and that He receives us as He receives His Son because it is He who has placed us 'in Him'!

The problem for most of us is that we don't take prayer seriously enough. Martin Luther was once asked what his plans were for the next day; his reply was, 'Work, work from early to late. In fact I have so much to do that I shall spend the first three hours in prayer.' Our practice may be the opposite. Our busyness may rule out prayer; whereas, in fact, it should make prayer all the more necessary. We may need to take ourselves in hand, and discipline ourselves more to pray. It's at this point that fasting - not necessarily as a regular habit but as an occasional exercise - comes into its own and has its place. Fasting concentrates the mind, and expresses that humble penitence before God which lies at the heart of all prayer, and especially when we've been convicted of our neglect of it. Fasting - as our Lord taught (Matt.6:16-18) - is a personal and private matter, but that makes it all the more important a subject to explore and use privately.

We can't exhaust prayer's potential and all that God is pleased to do by means of it. Crucial to our understanding of the Christian life is that God first created us and then redeemed us, in order that we might praise Him. Prayer in Jesus' Name always brings the kind of response expressed in Psalm 126: 3: 'The Lord has done great things for us, and we are filled with joy.' Prayers - as one of the Puritans put it - are the seeds of praises!

A prayer

Father, thank You that every time I've called to You, You've heard me, and saved me out of all my troubles. I'm ashamed that having given my testimony to Your many answers, I've then so often failed to pray when a new difficulty has arisen. Thank You for the privilege of praying in the Name of Your Son, Jesus Christ. Whenever I pray, help me to rest in His merits, and to pray in harmony with all He has revealed of Yourself. May my prayers be a reflection of my wonderful union with Him, and the authority of His Name. May the answers You give to my prayers serve to bring praise to You. For Jesus' sake. Amen.

4

Prayer And The Holy Spirit

Prayer without the Holy Spirit isn't true prayer at all. It would be folly to consider the subject of prayer, therefore, without giving careful thought to the Holy Spirit's essential involvement in our prayers. As the Third Person of the Trinity who lives in us as Christians, and who is the secret of the spiritual life the Lord Jesus Christ gives, the Spirit's work on our behalf includes active assistance in prayer. But that prompts a question.

To whom should we address our prayers

The Bible consistently teaches that the Person of the Father - as the First Person of the Trinity, and the source of power, grace and mercy - is the formal object of our prayers, the One to whom our prayers are normally directed. Our Lord Jesus Christ instructs us to pray. 'Our Father...' (Matthew 6: 9).

This calling upon God as Father is in the name of His Son, our Lord Jesus Christ, and with the aid of the Holy Spirit. The Lord Jesus is the one Mediator between God and man. When we put our trust in the Lord Jesus as our Mediator, we receive the Holy Spirit who conveys God's supplies of grace to us and enables us to do God's will.

Since the Holy Spirit is the Third Person of the Trinity and, therefore, divine, it's clearly appropriate to worship and adore Him, together with the Father and the Son, and for prayer to be offered to Him. But the Holy Spirit so identifies with us, and serves us, that He doesn't present Himself in the Bible as One to whom we are to direct our worship and our prayers. Rather the consistent pattern is that which Paul outlines in Ephesians 2: 18, where, writing of the Lord Jesus, Paul declares, 'For through him we have access to the Father by one Spirit.'

More than a clue

The Lord Jesus made a specific promise about the Holy Spirit immediately prior to His leaving His first disciples: 'I will ask the Father, and he will give you another Counsellor to be with you for ever - the Spirit of truth' (John 14: 16, 17). The words 'another Counsellor' provide more than a clue to the Holy Spirit's work on our behalf - in prayer and in much else besides. The Holy Spirit does for us what the Lord Jesus Himself did for His disciples - including prayer. Let's consider for a moment what the Lord Jesus did for His disciples with regard to prayer.

First, He taught His disciples to pray. He did it as a very deliberate exercise because of its importance. He encouraged them to ask in prayer that they might receive (Matthew 7: 7ff).

Second, He prayed for His disciples. He prayed for them as a group (John 17: 6ff), and He prayed for them individually (Luke 22: 32).

Third, He showed them by His example the place prayer should have in the life of all who serve God. The disciples found Him up early in the morning praying (Mark 1: 35; Luke 4: 42). They observed how He prayed before making important decisions, such as the calling and appointing of the apostles (Luke 6: 12, 13) and before crucial occasions, such as His questioning of the disciples about their convictions concerning His identity (Luke 9: 18; cf Matthew 16: 13). The Lord Jesus underlined the importance of prayer not only by His own consistent example, but also by His parables, and His plain teaching on the subject.

Fourth, the Lord Jesus prompted prayer. Looking out on the crowds, and seeing them 'harassed and helpless, like sheep without a shepherd' (Matthew 9: 36), He urged, 'Ask the Lord of the harvest... to send out workers into his harvest field' (Matthew 9:38). When He gave His disciples what we have come to know as 'the Lord's Prayer' He put words into their mouths, guiding them as to how they should pray.

Finally, the Lord Jesus helped the disciples in their prayers by His actual presence with them, by the influence His Person had upon the kind of things they wanted and desired. When He was with them, and they were listening to Him, they found themselves wanting and asking for the right things.

A most precious gift

The Holy Spirit, our promised Counsellor, does for us exactly what the Lord Jesus did for His disciples. He teaches us to pray, and He does so with determination. He is the Headmaster of God's school of prayer in which we all commence as 'beginners'. He regularly shows us the place prayer should have in the life of anyone who wants to serve God. Is there, for example, any effective Christian who hasn't been taught to pray, and who doesn't want to learn more in God's school of prayer?

The Holy Spirit teaches us the wisdom of making our decisions at God's throne of grace. He prompts prayer. He is able to give us eyes to see the crowds as Jesus saw them, so that we urgently pray for God's provision of harvesters for His harvest field. The Holy Spirit puts words and pleas into our mouths. By His presence within us, He influences our prayers and points them in the right direction. These are all benefits implied by our Lord's description of the Holy Spirit as 'another Counsellor'.

The Holy Spirit has been given to assist us in every aspect of our living of the Christian life. He increases our spiritual understanding; He gives spiritual strength and stamina; He guides and directs; and He provides gifts for service. He works both *in* and *with* us. But He is particularly our helper in prayer, and prayer is a non-event without His presence and activity. Responsible from the beginning for our spiritual new birth, the Holy Spirit helps us to utter our first cry to God - 'God, have mercy on me, a sinner' (Luke 18: 13; cf Acts 9: 11). As the Spirit of adoption, He makes it natural for us to cry, 'Abba, Father'. He testifies with our spirit that we are God's children (Romans 8: 16) and this assurance helps us to pray with a real measure of confidence, in harmony with reverence for our heavenly Father.

Besides helping us to pray, the Holy Spirit also prompts prayer. Acts 13 describes a radical new departure, so far as the spread of the gospel was concerned, in the history of the early Church. The early Christians obviously felt the burden of the unevangelised Gentile world. There's no doubt that God the Holy Spirit prompted the Christians in Antioch that day to meet together to worship and fast, as they sought God's will concerning the fulfilment of their responsibility to those who hadn't heard the good news of Jesus. Having prompted them to pray, God the Holy Spirit directed them as to God's answer: 'While they were worshipping the Lord and fasting, the Holy Spirit said, "Set apart for me Barnabas and Saul for the work to which I have called them". So after they had fasted and prayed, they placed their hands on them and sent them off. The two of them, sent on their way by the Holy Spirit, went down to Seleucia...' (Acts 13: 2-4).

A few chapters later, we find Paul and Silas in prison in the Roman colony of Philippi, with their backs bleeding after a severe and totally undeserved flogging. Luke records that 'About midnight Paul and Silas were praying and singing hymns to God, and the other prisoners were listening to them' (Acts 16: 25). God the Holy Spirit, the Counsellor, had come alongside them, and He prompted them to pray and to praise God. The Holy Spirit prompts us to pray, likewise, even in the most severe adversity, for it's then that we often need to pray most. He is the unique inspirer of prayer.

There will be times, too, when we find the Holy Spirit prompting us to pray for particular individuals. It may be presumptuous at the time to describe it as the Spirit prompting, but looking back afterwards we may often be in no doubt that it was His work because we discover just how amazingly timely our prayers were. In the course of a day, someone's name or face may come to mind for no apparent reason, and it may be that of someone thousands of miles away, with whom no immediate communication is possible. Only time may tell whether or not that awareness of the other person is the Spirit's prompting to pray, but it will always be right to follow through that possible prompting with prayer, and, at the same time, to ask the Holy Spirit's guidance to know how to pray. We should respond to every impulse to pray as a matter of habit, whether we are walking along the street, driving our car, doing our daily work, or reading our Bible. Any call to prayer which we sense we are receiving should never be thought of as a distraction.

Having prompted prayer, the Holy Spirit will guide us as to the best time or times in the day to pray. We're all different in our circumstances and temperaments. The best time in the day to pray is quite different for the mother of young children than for the single person who does a nine-to-five type of job.

The Holy Spirit also delights to guide our prayers so that they are acceptable to God. His activity at this point is varied. He guides our prayers so that they are geared to the glory of God. The phrase 'the glory of God' may easily trip off our tongues and not mean much. But the Holy Spirit wants the glory of God to mean everything to us. The things which are to God's glory are the matters which bring honour to Him, and which exhibit in some way the wonder of all that God is, and all He has shown Himself to be in His Son Jesus Christ. The Holy Spirit helps us to subordinate our desires to God's glory, to help us want what pleases God most of all. Without the Spirit's aid, we would tend to aim to please ourselves.

To achieve this purpose of our praying with God's glory in view, the Holy Spirit informs our minds so that we recognise the benefits for which we should pray. The Holy Spirit always respects our minds. As our minds are renewed, our way of thinking is transformed so that we increasingly want to do God's will because we know it is 'good, pleasing and perfect' (Romans 12: 2).

The Holy Spirit reveals those aspects of God's character and benefits which especially arouse our love for God - His goodness, His mercy, the grace, the love and the glory of the Lord Jesus, and the riches of God's promises. He then stirs up in us the appropriate feelings and response to the truths He has taught us about God our Father and His Son, our Saviour. Having given us right views of God, He brings to mind God's many promises, prompting us to pray for the things of which God approves, for the benefits which it's God's purpose to give. He keeps a check on our requests so that they coincide with God's purposes of holiness for our life. He helps us to pray according to the mind of God, something we don't know how to do left to ourselves.

Wisdom to stop and start

The Holy Spirit provides wisdom to know when to stop praying. I find that when I am seeking to determine God's will about something, I may sometimes feel the need to pray a number of times concerning it, especially if I'm finding my submission to God's will in the matter difficult to achieve. But there comes a point when to pray about the subject any further would be an act of unbelief, a suggestion on my part that God hasn't heard. The Holy Spirit, in His own unique and almost indefinable way, makes us aware of that key moment when to pray any more about the matter would be wrong. In certain situations the Holy Spirit may give a quiet and deep assurance that our prayers are answered, and that there's no more need for prayer but rather for praise. We can't easily explain these moments of understanding to others, and how they arise, but we've no doubt of their reality as we progress in the school and discipline of prayer.

On the other hand, the Holy Spirit gives wisdom to know when to pray, and for what to pray. In particular, the Holy Spirit provides the wisdom promised in James 1: 5, especially in knowing how to pray about our trials. Human wisdom would incline us to pray, 'Lord, help me to escape'. Spiritual wisdom, however, will rather cause us to cry to God, 'Lord, let the testing of my faith through this trial produce perseverance, as You promise, and let perseverance finish its work so that I may be mature and complete, not lacking anything in my character that You want for me' (see James 1: 3, 4).

The Holy Spirit guides, and provides His wisdom, most of all, by means of the understanding He gives us of His Word, the Scriptures, and especially through the accumulated understanding we gain over the months and years of our Christian experience. He has a unique capacity to bring to mind just the Scripture we need which will guide us and give light where we are in darkness.

Let's consider two familiar examples. As our Lord Jesus Christ approached the Cross, He was distressed in soul at the dreadful prospect of becoming sin for us. John records His words, and His prayer to His Father: 'Now my heart is troubled, and what shall I say "Father, save me from this hour"? No, it was for this very reason I came to this hour. Father, glorify your name!' (John 12:27, 28). The natural disturbance of spirit which the prospect of the Cross brought so distressed our Lord that His immediate and natural reaction was to escape from it. But then there came to His mind - and anointed by the Spirit as He was, we must clearly recognise the Spirit's influence here - the remembrance of His Father's will, and all that the Father promised to achieve by His Son's obedience, so He prayed, 'Father, glorify your name' - the best of prayers.

We've mentioned earlier that the apostle Paul had what he described as a 'thorn in my flesh, a messenger of Satan' (2 Corinthians 12: 7), the word 'flesh' implying that it was some kind of physical disability. Convinced that he could serve God better without it, Paul pleaded for its removal - and he did so three times, so acutely did he feel the burden of it. But the Lord said to Paul, 'My grace is sufficient for you, for my power is made perfect in weakness' (2 Corinthians 12: 9). Did Paul actually hear the Lord's voice saying this? Or was it God the Holy Spirit bringing to bear upon Paul's situation the words and promises of the Old Testament and the teaching of the Lord Jesus, so that Paul here sums up in one sentence what the Lord said to him through the testimony of Scripture. Whatever the answer, the understanding given to Paul caused him to change his prayer! Instead of looking for the removal of 'the thorn', he looked for Christ's power to rest on him the more, so as to demonstrate the truth of what the Lord had promised him about his weakness (2 Corinthians 12:9).

The manner in which the Holy Spirit brings Scriptures to our minds as we pray - and sometimes Scriptures we haven't read for a long while - is invaluable and often remarkable. He loves to make us aware of the different ways in which God's grace and peace are promised to us so that we may live our lives enjoying these priceless benefits.

The Spirit's intercession- different from that of our Lord Jesus Christ

The Holy Spirit intercedes for us: 'the Spirit helps us in our weakness. We do not know what we ought to pray, but the Spirit himself intercedes for us with groans that words cannot express. And he who searches our hearts knows the mind of the Spirit, because the Spirit intercedes for the saints in accordance with God's will' (Romans 8: 26, 27). Since these verses constitute the sole statement on the subject, certain limits are immediately imposed upon our understanding of them. Furthermore, Romans 8 also tells us that our Lord Jesus is 'at the right hand of God and is also interceding for us' (34). This statement is paralleled in Hebrews 7: 25 where we're told that He 'always lives to intercede' for us. But there's clearly a difference between the intercession of the Lord Jesus as our High Priest in heaven, and the intercession of the Holy Spirit within us.

First, the Lord Jesus Christ presents His own merits; the Holy Spirit does not present any merits of His own. As our righteous Substitute, the Lord Jesus suffered for us on the Cross, and as our worthy Representative, He appears in heaven to claim our deliverance. His intercession has to do primarily with the restoration and reconciliation of sinners to God through His Cross, so that what the Holy Spirit accomplishes on earth in believers' hearts the Lord Jesus pleads in heaven (cf John 17: 20). His intercession has regard to His people both before and after their entry into salvation.

Secondly, the Lord Jesus asks in His own name; the Holy Spirit, however, asks nothing in His own name. Because He, the Son of God, has been given the name Saviour - 'you are to give him the name Jesus, because he will save his people from their sins' (Matthew 1: 21) - and He has accomplished His people's salvation, a fact testified to by His resurrection and ascension, He is able to ask in His own name. He asks that His people should be brought safely home to God, that their sins committed after conversion should be forgiven them, and that all the help of God's Spirit should be given them day by day until they finally arrive in God's heavenly home and kingdom.

Thirdly, our Lord Jesus reigns in heaven, and His intercession secures our prayers' acceptance; the Holy Spirit, on the other hand, lives in us who offer the prayers, providing us with the assistance we need. He prompts us to offer them, and assists us in doing so, but they are not His but ours.

The distinction may be the better appreciated as we consider the use of the word 'Advocate', a title given to both our Lord and the Holy Spirit. An advocate does two things: first, he stands and pleads on behalf of his client; secondly, he advises his client how to speak when he has to do so. Our Lord Jesus Christ acts for us in the first sense: He appears in God's presence on our behalf, interceding by His own presence there and on the basis of His finished work on the Cross. His intercession underlines the perpetual effectiveness of His sacrifice, and its continual application to all who believe. The Holy Spirit acts for us in the second sense: He puts pleas and words in our mouths. The Lord Jesus as our Advocate makes intercession *for* us in heaven (Romans 8: 34); the Holy Spirit as our advocate makes intercession *within* us, helping us to put our prayers into words, stirring up our desires for what is in accord with God's will.

We have to ask a question at this point which we probably can't answer with any certainty. Does this mention of the Spirit's intercession mean that He prays for us independently of our prayers? On the slender evidence of this one statement in Romans 8: 26, 27 on the subject, I think the answer is most likely 'No'. The implication is that the Holy Spirit helps us *as we pray,* sympathetically aware as He is of our weakness. His intercession is made not as our substitute but as our helper. He prays only in the hearts of those Christians who pray. He intercedes in us and by us. What He does, He does in and for us. He helps us to recognise our need, and to turn our desires into longings and groanings which God will delight to answer. We may make the simple yet powerful cry, 'Lord, help me!' and He turns that general prayer into a specific request for the help we need. Without our realising it, He puts requests and words into our mouths, not as His, but as our own. As He excites our feelings, He also enables us to give expression to them in the right manner: He intercedes for us in accordance with God's will. The Holy Spirit's intercession expresses His complete identification with us. He comes alongside us when we are weak or overwhelmed, and He bears the burden with us, until we cast it effectively upon the Lord Himself. He interprets our inarticulate groans and turns them into effective prayer.

Praying in the Spirit

We are twice instructed to 'pray in the Spirit'. At the conclusion of his instruction concerning the Christian's armour and weapons, Paul urges, 'And pray in the Spirit on all occasions with all kinds of prayers and requests' (Ephesians 6: 18). Jude similarly encourages his readers, '...and pray in the Holy Spirit' (Jude 20). While it's helpful to attempt a definition and explanation of 'praying in the Spirit', we must remember that the Scriptures nowhere do so.

First, praying in the Holy Spirit is obviously something vital, and not mechanical. He is the Third Person of the Living God, and the Spirit of life and power. Prayer in the Spirit always reflects His life and power.

Second, to pray in the Spirit is the opposite of hypocrisy since He is the Spirit of truth. Our prayers mustn't come simply from our lips but from the bottom of our hearts, and they do so when we pray 'in the Spirit'.

Third, to pray in the Spirit is to pray in dependence upon His help, appreciating our helplessness in prayer without Him.

Fourth, to pray in the Spirit is to be assured of our access into God's presence as we come in the appointed way through our Lord Jesus Christ. The Holy Spirit delights to assure us of our acceptance with God, to make us keenly and joyfully aware that we are in God's presence, and that there are no obstructions to our coming to the throne of grace.

Fifth, to pray in the Spirit is to be filled with the Spirit as we pray. Filled with the Spirit, we are under His control and we're guided in our requests by what He has taught us, especially through the Scriptures. Filled by the Spirit, we are led by the Spirit, in our prayers as in everything else (Galatians 5: 18) - He is the guide and master of our prayers. To pray in the Spirit, therefore, is to pray with the concerns of the Spirit foremost - the glory of the Lord Jesus, our own sanctification, and the needs of people who are without God and without Christ in the world.

Prayer in the Spirit is the most effective weapon there is against Satan. When we take up the Spirit's sword, the Scriptures, and use the weapon of prayer with the Spirit's full support, we are invincible in our service of God in the world. No wonder Satan does everything he can either to stop us praying or to cause us to grieve or quench the Spirit.

We may well ask the question, 'How do we know if we are praying in the Spirit?' What we have considered already provides the clues. We may give three answers.

First, when we pray in the Spirit we clearly want to do so. No one prays in the Spirit without the desire. Certainly it is the Spirit Himself who prompts the desire, but we will know the desire at the same time to be our own.

Second, when we pray in the Spirit we will be aware that the things we ask are in accord with God's will: they will be essentially pure and spiritual, and not selfish and grasping in nature. Often the things we ask for will be blessings we are commanded and encouraged in the Scriptures to want, and, if not, they will be benefits in keeping with the general teaching of Scripture.

Third, when we pray in the Spirit the consequence will be an experience of God's peace, and an attitude of complete submission to God, no matter how He may choose to answer our prayers.

SOS

The Holy Spirit wants us to live out in practice the life of intimate fellowship with God which is our spiritual birthright. When we are in any kind of spiritual difficulty, we should make an urgent appeal to the Holy Spirit for His assistance - and this we do by prayer, and by asking for His help in prayer.

We can probably identify circumstances or periods in our lives when prayer has been particularly hard-going. I find that I'm very sluggish in prayer when I'm physically or emotionally tired. When I spent a brief period in hospital, having seemingly all the time in the world to pray, I found it difficult to pray because there was always so much going on, and it was impossible to obtain the quietness I usually associate with the times when I pray at home. Bereavement, too, can be a difficult time for the exercise of prayer. A kind of emotional numbness may descend upon us.

One of the wonderful things about Christian fellowship is that when we aren't able to pray for ourselves easily, God raises up others who pray for us. Nevertheless, no matter how difficult our circumstances, and contradictory our feelings, it's always appropriate to call to God for the help of His Spirit. When the Spirit simply helps us to cry the word 'Father!' as a plea for help, like a child calling out in the middle of the night for its parents' help, that one word is sufficient. But so often as soon as we call to God for the Spirit's help, we find the Spirit present with His powerful assistance. And this has always been the case.

Although the language is old-fashioned, William Gurnall, one of the Puritan writers, puts it well: 'Whence then must the fire come to thaw the iciness of the heart, but from heaven? The Spirit, He must stretch Himself upon the soul, as the prophet on the child, and then the soul will come to some kindly warmth and heavenly heat in its affections. The Spirit must groan, and then the soul will groan. He helps us to these signs and groans which turn the sails of prayer. He dissolves the heart, and then it (i.e. prayer) bursts out of the heart by groans of the lips by heavenly rhetoric, out of the eyes as from a flood-gate of tears.'

A necessary caution

We may find ourselves knowing little of the Spirit's assistance in prayer, and we must be honest enough to ask 'Why?' if we want to make progress.

The first reason may be that we've been ignorant of what to expect the Holy Spirit to do for us. Knowledge and experience go hand in hand in Christian experience. If we don't *understand* what God promises, we may not *experience* what He promises. This explains God's provision of His Word and teachers of His Word. God reveals and teaches us what He wants us to know and enjoy of His goodness.

Second, we may not have asked God for His Spirit's help in prayer. Knowledge plus faith equals Christian experience. God wants us to ask Him specifically for the Spirit's help. As the Lord Jesus Himself said, 'If you then, though you are evil, know how to give good gifts to your children, how much more will your Father in heaven give the Holy Spirit to those who ask him!' (Luke 11: 13). Faith and asking are inseparable, and to please God we must exercise faith. Part of the exercise of faith is requesting the Spirit's help as we pray.

Third, we may grieve or quench the Holy Spirit and thus restrict His beneficial activity on our behalf, not only in prayer, but particularly in prayer. We grieve the Holy Spirit (Ephesians 4: 30), by sinful and unChristlike behaviour. If we're disobedient to God's will (Isaiah 1: 15-17; 59: 1f; Deuteronomy 1: 43-45), loveless (Isaiah 58: 3-10), unjust (Micah 3: 1 f) and unforgiving (Ephesians 4: 32), we'll find our experience of the Spirit's help either restricted or totally withdrawn.

Peter writes of a husband's prayers being hindered if he doesn't treat his wife with consideration (1 Peter 3: 7), and the removal of the Spirit's help is no doubt the reason why his prayers will be hindered. James writes of 'the prayer of a righteous man' being 'powerful and effective' (James 5: 16). 'A righteous man' is a believer whose life proves his faith, who lives in such a way that his experience of the Holy Spirit's assistance is unrestricted. The Holy Spirit is quenched when we resist His influence in our lives, especially as He communicates God's will, and Word to us through His appointed agents or messengers (1 Thessalonians 5: 19, 20).

There's an undoubted relationship between our hearing and obeying God's Word - every time we either read it or receive it through teaching and preaching - and our ability to pray in the Spirit with His maximum help. The proper exercise of prayer can't be separated from the proper obedience which is at the heart of the Christian life. Every time I resist God's Word, or pretend that He isn't speaking to me on some particularly sensitive subject or issue of obedience, I pour water on the Spirit's fire within me. How foolish to hinder the activity of the Holy Spirit, our perfect Counsellor!

Pray!

In another context, Paul instructed Timothy 'to fan into flame the gift of God' which was in him (2 Timothy 1: 6), a reference to the special anointing of the Spirit Timothy received when he had been set apart for the Christian ministry. But the instruction has relevance to God's gift of the Spirit to us in relation to prayer. We won't know the Spirit's help by simply waiting for it. We won't know the Spirit's assistance in prayer by simply waiting until we feel like praying. We will know His help as we pray. It's in praying that He comes alongside us with His invaluable and amazing assistance. As we turn to prayer, no matter how impossible it sometimes seems, we'll find the flames of the Spirit fanned, and bursting forth into fervent and effective prayer.

We couldn't have any greater encouragement to pray than God already gives us. God our Father is willing to hear our prayers. The Lord Jesus is our Advocate, willing to present our requests in the court of heaven. And the Holy Spirit, our personal Secretary, is always at hand, willing to suggest and to draw up our requests. What greater encouragement could we want?

A prayer

Heavenly Father, thank You that You did not spare Your own Son, but gave Him up for us all, and that along with Him, You graciously give us so many wonderful gifts. Thank You for the precious gift of the Holy Spirit to inhabit our lives and to make real our experience of the salvation You give us in Your Son.

Please forgive me for those times and occasions when I have grieved or quenched Him. Make me sensitive to anything which displeases Him as He seeks to make me holy and useful to You.

From now on I want to realise my dependence on the Holy Spirit every time I pray, and I long to know all the assistance He can give me. When I find prayer difficult, cause me to remember that it is in praying that He will come alongside me. Even now I would fan the fires of Your Spirit, and trust You for His moment by moment support and direction. In Jesus' Name, I pray. Amen.

5
Method in prayer

Method isn't unspiritual. A myth does the rounds from time to time that method - or anything resembling it - is somehow or other in conflict with the freedom the Holy Spirit gives in prayer. Some of the Christians in Corinth fell into the snare of imagining that order and method conflicted with the Holy Spirit's activity and control among them. Paul reminded them that 'God is not a God of disorder' and that 'everything should be done in a fitting and orderly way' (1 Corinthians 14: 33, 40), and that this instruction wasn't at all in conflict with the freedom the Spirit gives.

A method is a way of doing something, which has already proved helpful in achieving an end. Bishop George Reindorp tells of a nurse who helped a patient by sharing with him how she prayed using her right hand to provide the agenda. As her thumb was nearest to her, she prayed for those who were nearest to her, all those she loved wherever they were. The next finger, the one used at school by the teacher when she was wanted, reminded her to pray for all those who taught her in any way. Then the third finger, the tallest, stood for the VIPs, and she prayed for the Queen and those in authority in the nations. If you have tried to play the piano, you will know that the fourth finger is the weakest of them all. So she then prayed for the unwell and those in need. When she came to the little finger, which is perhaps the least important, she prayed for herself in her work and her needs. Any such simple organisation of this nature is a great help. Having such a system, we can turn to good purpose the odd moments which come to us in travelling or waiting for an appointment.

Imagine having a meeting with a person of influence

from whom you desire help. Your intention and purpose would be to gain the maximum benefit from the interview. It would be a matter of courtesy to the person concerned, and to your advantage, to have thought out beforehand exactly what you wanted to ask, and the order of priority. You would probably write your request down beforehand, drawing up an agenda. To introduce such method into our praying isn't at all in conflict with our dependence upon the Holy Spirit. He is the one - our Secretary - who will help us to draw up the agenda and then present with us, our requests, to the throne of grace. The Holy Spirit delights in order and purposefulness on our part because they show that we mean business. While prayer is subject to inspiration, it requires intelligence (1 Cor. 14: 15).

Time and place

Method begins with discovering the right time to pray, and the best place. Our Lord Jesus Christ set us an example of method. First thing in the day, rising early, He sought out a quiet place, away from interruption. The only way He could get such undisturbed times was by getting up a good while before others. Once the world was awake, people were seeking Him out for His help and His teaching. Mark describes our Lord's pattern and method: 'Very early in the morning, while it was still dark, Jesus got up, left the house and went off to a solitary place, where he prayed' (Mark 1: 35; cf 3: 13; Luke 6: 12). When staying in Jerusalem, the Mount of Olives seems to have been our Lord's favourite place for prayer (Luke 22: 39).

Because habit plays such an important part in our lives, a familiar place - a room, or kneeling at a chair - helps us to get quickly into the atmosphere of prayer. Luke tells us that Peter 'went up on the roof to pray' (Acts 10: 9), and there's little doubt that this was because it was a place of quietness for undisturbed prayer. 'When you pray,' Jesus taught, 'go into your room, close the door and pray to your

Father, who is unseen' (Matthew 6: 6). Young people who have to share a bedroom, may find privacy difficult to obtain. A father wanting quiet before he goes off to work may find it almost impossible most days when there are children to be dressed, fed and got off to school. But where there's a will, there's a way. An office-worker found that the answer was to get into work half an hour before work began when he could have his office to himself, in order to read his Bible and pray. Another friend found that the answer - working in a city as he did - was to slip into a church that was open during the lunch-hour, and sit quietly and pray.

Method is also relevant when it comes to determining when and how often we pray in the day. Although Daniel set a helpful example of praying three times a day, no law is laid down as to how many times in a day we should pray. As John Newton put it many years ago:

'Daniel prayed three times a-day; which the Psalmist speaks of as his practice likewise; and in one place declares his purpose of praising God seven times a-day. This last expression is perhaps indefinite, not precisely seven times, but very often. Indeed a person who lives in the exercise of faith and love, and who finds by experience that it is good for him to draw nigh to God, will not want to be told how often he must pray, any more than how often he must converse with an earthly friend.'

The important thing is to determine for ourselves what is the best time for us personally. Our circumstances vary so much. The mother of young children, for example, will seldom be able to have a set time of prayer early in the morning because her baby and young children will demand her attention often even before she awakes! But there will be moments in the day - no matter how brief - when time for prayer can be found. It may be while feeding the baby, or when the children have a sleep during the day or when they are put to bed at night. The pattern of life is different for all of us, but there's always a time that is right for us personally if we'll honestly look for it. And it's obviously important that we find it. Calvin put it well:

'Because almost the whole day we are distracted by a variety of occupations, and we are constantly bustling about unless we hold ourselves in check by applying the bridle, it is useful to have hours set apart for prayer, not because we are tied down to hours, but so that prayer may not escape our memory when it ought to take priority over all our concerns.'

For most of us the morning is the best time for our main time of prayer since it's likely then that we are at our freshest and most alert - so long as we have gone to bed at a reasonable time. Part of the discipline of the Christian life is regulating not only the time we get up but the time we go to bed. No one manages to give prayer its proper place without discipline: 'Morning by morning, O Lord, you hear my voice; morning by morning I lay my requests before you and wait in expectation', David declared to the Lord (Psalm 5:3). David's life was that of a busy king, and he knew the value of spreading every new day before God. If we find the best time is the evening, then we must ensure that we don't leave it too late so that we're over-tired. The time we ought to give to prayer is more important than the timing of the end of a television programme that is particularly attractive and in conflict with our prayer pattern. In his *Prayer: Letters to Malcolm* , C S Lewis wrote:

'... no one in his senses ... would reserve his chief prayers for bed-time - obviously the worst possible hour for any action which needs concentration... My own plan, when hard pressed, is to seize any time, and place, however unsuitable, in preference to the last waking moment. On a day of travelling - with, perhaps, some ghastly meeting at the end of it - I'd rather pray sitting in a crowded train than put it off till midnight when one reaches a hotel bedroom with aching head and dry throat and one's mind partly in a stupor and partly in a whirl. On other, and slightly less crowded days, a bench in a park, or a back street where one can pace up and down, will do.'

The timing of our times of prayer is a personal matter, and one for personal decision. But we won't make much progress unless we honestly ask, 'When is the best time for me to pray? and where?' As we then follow the most suitable pattern, our resolution to give appropriate time to prayer produces results. It's unhelpful to pray watching the clock, feeling that if we've prayed for fifteen minutes or half-an-hour that we've somehow or other done our duty. In prayer our foremost aim is to meet with God, to acknowledge Him and to spread our needs, and those of others, before Him. When we've done that, we've prayed long enough, no matter how many hours or how few minutes we've taken.

Prayer and Bible reading- which should come first?

Method is relevant in the relationship of prayer to Bible reading. However there's no rule given by God in the Bible which says that one must come before the other. Prayer is always appropriate before we read the Bible in that we need to pray for the Holy Spirit's illumination. As a sundial is dependent upon the sun to be effective, so we're dependent upon the Holy Spirit if the Scriptures are going to mean to us what God intends. David's prayer - or a prayer like it - is always in place: 'Open my eyes that I may see wonderful things in your law' (Psalm 119: 18).

There have been occasions when I've struggled to understand a passage with little progress only to realise that I've not asked for the Holy Spirit's help. Having rectified that, understanding has come.

On the other hand, there's much to be said for our main period of prayer and intercession arising from our Bible reading. It's even more important to let God speak to us, than for us to speak to Him. Furthermore, when He speaks to us by His Word, we can properly respond to Him, answer Him and seek His direction in a positive and intelligent way. George Muller's testimony may help us:

'Formerly, when I rose, I began to pray as soon as possible, and generally spent all my time till breakfast in prayer, or almost all the time... But what was the result? I often spent a quarter of an hour, or half an hour, or even an hour on my knees, before being conscious to myself of having derived comfort, encouragement, humbling of soul, etc; and often, after having suffered much from wandering of mind for the first ten minutes, or a quarter of an hour, or even half an hour, I only then began *really to pray* . I scarcely ever suffer now in this way. For my heart being nourished by the truth, being brought into *experimental* fellowship with God, I speak to my Father, and to my Friend (vile though I am and unworthy of it!) about the things that He has brought before me in His precious Word.'

An outstanding benefit of prayer after reading the Bible is that it helps to maintain our freshness in prayer and to avoid unhelpful ruts. As we respond every day to what God says to us in His Word, our requests take a different form each day, as His Word prompts the agenda. I've been reading Paul's first letter to Timothy in my daily reading, and that's provided a helpful guide to the kind of requests I should make. For example, 1 Timothy 2: 1-7 was Monday's passage with the instruction to pray for everyone because of God's desire for all men and women to be saved and to come to a knowledge of the truth. The specific instruction is also given to pray for kings and all those in authority. While I pray for these things fairly frequently, it was right to pray for them in a most deliberate way on Monday, reminding myself as I did so that there's an urgent need for all to be reconciled to God and there's only one Mediator between God and men, the man Christ Jesus. The next day the passage was 1 Timothy 2: 8-15, a passage which has a bearing on modern issues such as the place of women in the Church, and the important subject of feminism. It was good to be prompted to pray for wisdom in understanding God's will in these matters, and for obedience to His will. In this way, prayer is kept fresh as we make it part of our habit and method to respond to God as He speaks to us through His Word.

If we read the Bible systematically - a practice to be highly recommended - there will be times when we read a part which may not readily speak to us. It may be a passage in Leviticus, or a chapter in one of the historical books which is basically a list of names. I find it helpful in such cases to read not only that passage but to read on, or to be systematically reading another Bible book like the book of Psalms at the same time, so that I can read there until I find something that speaks to me and guides me either as to the way in which I should praise God today or respond to His will.

Whether we use their Bible Reading Notes or not, what is commonly known as the Scripture Union Method is as much a help to prayer as it is to Bible reading. The Scripture Union Method means asking the following questions of every passage:

1) What does this passage teach us about God - the Father, His Son Jesus Christ, or the Holy Spirit?

2) What does this passage teach us about the Christian life?

For example, is there:

a) A command, a promise or a warning?
b) An example to follow or an error to avoid?
3) What is the main lesson?

When we have some answer to give to Question 1, we'll always have something for which to praise and worship God - and in a constant variety of ways. When we answer Question 2, we'll find ourselves responding in obedience, and asking for the assistance of God's Spirit to work it out in us. When we determine in Question 3 what the main lesson is, we'll have a necessary topic for meditation before God in prayer, and that in turn will lead to specific and practical obedience.

The danger of the great variety of Bible reading aids available is that we may read them more than we read the Bible, and we may leave them to do the work for us. Instead of our asking the right questions of the Bible passage we're reading, we may leave it to the author of the notes that we use. Such a practice seldom leads to the fresh, spontaneous and meaningful prayer which personal exposure to the passage brings. Now the use of Bible Reading Notes needn't have this effect; but it's a snare to avoid.

Prayer's parts

Is there a right order to follow as we pray? Should there be a structure about our prayers? Behind questions such as these there's the thought that adoration of God, for example, should come before thanksgiving, and that confession of sin should come before making our requests to God. There is a natural order, and it has been expressed in a number of ways to help our memories. The most familiar is probably the use of the word *ACTS* , being the first letters of the words, Adoration, Confession, Thanksgiving and Supplication. Such a suggested order is fine so long as it remains a guide and doesn't become a spiritual strait-jacket.

Adoration of God is obviously the appropriate place to begin. But we may not always feel able to begin in this manner. We may be so overwhelmed by a sense of failure and sin that we're totally unable to praise God until we've put things right with Him. John Newton expressed this need in one of his hymns, the first line of which is, 'Come, my soul, thy suit prepare... ' and which has the following prayer in its third verse:

'With my burden I begin;
Lord, remove this load of sin!
Let Thy blood for sinners spilt
Set my conscience free from guilt.'

While, hopefully, we'll not have to begin too frequently in this manner, to hold fast to *ACTS* when our feelings match those of John Newton would be most artificial and probably not true prayer at all. To know of prayer's different parts should assist us rather than daunt us.

The Lord's Prayer

There's a debate sometimes as to whether the Lord's Prayer is a prayer to be prayed together as God's family or whether it was given purely and simply as a guide and pattern. Our Lord Himself didn't say, and we've no means of answering the question authoritatively. The most satisfactory answer is that it was given both as a family prayer, to be prayed as often as thought appropriate, and as a pattern prayer - with the latter purpose to the fore. If ever we feel that we're praying the Lord's Prayer together in a purely mechanical and unthinking way then we'll be wise to stop using it for a while, and then come back to it with freshness. On the other hand, if we use the words from our hearts, it's a delightful way of expressing our corporate concern for the interests of our heavenly Father's kingdom and family.

There are six basic parts to the Lord's Prayer: the first three are concerned principally with God, and the remaining three with our personal needs and interests - that immediately suggests the kind of balance which we should endeavour to strike.

Our first concern must be for God's own name and glory: 'Our Father in heaven, hallowed be your name' (Matthew 6: 9). This prayer expresses our desire that men and women everywhere may know the truth about God, and respect and love Him; and that those who claim a relationship with Him may live in a way that brings praise to Him.

Our second concern must be for the coming of His kingdom: 'your kingdom come' (Matthew 6: 10). This prayer expresses our concern that the number of those who believe in God's Son and enter His kingdom may increase day by day, so that His Son's return may be brought forward.

Our third concern must be for the doing of God's will in the world: 'your will be done on earth as it is in heaven' (Matthew 6: 10). In this prayer we pray for our own obedience, as well as the obedience of men and women everywhere to the purposes of God, and the doing of His will in spite of our frequent disobedience and misapprehension of His will.

Having given priority to the things that relate to God Himself, we may pray for ourselves with confidence, because God, through the Lord Jesus' saving work, has become our heavenly Father.

First, we are encouraged to pray for our daily bread: 'Give us today our daily bread' (Matthew 6: 11). This prayer symbolises and represents all our daily needs - food, clothing, housing and everything relating to our physical and material well-being, and to our daily employment.

Second, as much as we require our daily bread, we

need daily forgiveness: 'Forgive us our debts, as we also have forgiven our debtors' (Matthew 6: 12). Our forgiving of others their sins against us is not a form of merit that earns our forgiveness from God; but the reality of our experience of God's forgiveness proves itself in the practice of forgiveness on our part; and our continuing experience of God's forgiveness depends upon our reflecting His forgiveness in our personal relationships. Human relationships - being so important to us - are to figure prominently in our prayers and intercessions.

Then, finally, we need to seek God's help against temptation and our enemy, the devil: 'And lead us not into temptation but deliver us from the evil one' (Luke 11:4). Satan, our great spiritual enemy, is always on the prowl, like a roaring lion, looking for someone to trip up by evil and temptation.

The Lord's Prayer provides us with a skeleton agenda upon which we may put 'flesh' according to our immediate understanding of urgent needs and our own situation. We should pray regularly for:

1) The honour of God's Name in the world.

2) The extension of the Church and the coming of God's kingdom through the preaching of the gospel.

3) The obedience of God's people to God's will, and God's overruling control of all the events of the world.

4) Our daily practical needs and our work.

5) Our relationships, both with God and others, and their maintenance through the experience of forgiveness.

6) Our temptations and the spiritual battle in which all Christians are involved.

Other Bible prayers may also assist us. The book of Psalms is crammed full of prayers, and we'll find this order, so clearly set out in the Lord's Prayer, reflected there. In addition, we have the prayers of the apostle Paul in his New Testament letters.

On being practical

We must never forget that personality enters into our practice of prayer as into everything else. What may be helpful and practical to some may not be the same for others. The important thing is to find what's best for oneself. I'll share my own experience, not with the intention of suggesting that it will be the best for you, but in order to stimulate you to find out the best method for yourself if you haven't yet discovered it.

I have what I call my 'prayer diary'. It's a small loose-leaf book which can take a good number of pages, and it's made up of three parts. First, there's a page which lists urgent needs. This page is regularly updated or replaced. Second, there are seven pages, one for each day of the week, on which I write the names of people, and matters of concern. Third, there are thirty-one pages for the days of an average month to assist me in praying monthly for others whom I know and for whom I feel a concern. At the beginning of a new year I review the whole of my prayer diary, sometimes rewriting it. The benefit of using a loose-leaf book, however, is that it can be reviewed, changed and amended as the year goes on without having to rewrite the whole diary. I find it an invaluable asset to private prayer.

On the pages of the days of each week, I may write down regular events that occur on certain days so that I remember to pray for them. The names of people for whom I feel a particular responsibility are also written down there. Over the years I have gathered so many friends - and not least friends who are missionaries; these and others are found in my prayer diary so that I pray for them once a month.

On the weekly pages, I've taken the six points we've identified from the Lord's Prayer and put one down for each day in order, omitting Tuesday, commencing with Sunday. The reason I've left out Tuesday is that it's my 'day off', and so as not to get into a rut I often pray on a Tuesday without using my prayer diary.

Let me share a few other things I've found helpful. At times I find my praise and worship of God don't flow as they ought, or I feel I'm using the same words without freshness. It's a helpful exercise to put at the top of each weekly page of the prayer diary some attribute or characteristic of God for which you can praise and thank Him. That means that you will praise Him in a different way on Sunday than on Monday, and so on. In addition, every time I come across a Scripture which stirs me up to praise God, or presents a promise which is especially meaningful, I write it out in full under one of the page headings for one of the days of the month. I find this adds freshness to my worship and my petitions.

It may be helpful to think of the Lord's Prayer as an example of the kind of agenda we should have before us, already prepared, when we begin to pray. I found myself greatly challenged concerning this in reading the biography of James O Fraser, a pioneer missionary among the Lisu people of Yunnan in China, who wrote:

'I find it well to preface prayer not only by meditation but by the definite request that I may be directed into the channels of prayer to which the Holy Spirit is beckoning me. I also find it helpful to make a short list, like notes prepared for a sermon, before every season of prayer. The mind needs to be guided as well as the spirit attuned. I can thus get my thoughts in order, and having prepared my prayer can put the notes on the table or chair before me, kneel down and get to business.'

That kind of practice is unlikely to be necessary or practical every day, but there are undoubtedly times when such a preparation will not only prove helpful but also show how seriously we take prayer, and the importance we attach to it.

Praying aloud

We can pray without using our lips and our tongue, and we often practise prayer like this when we are travelling, or sending up an SOS to God in the course of our daily work. But in our regular times of private prayer most of us will probably find it a tremendous aid to pray aloud - providing, of course, there's no other person sharing the room or place! Prayer is to be as natural as conversation, and when we talk with others we use our voice. For prayer to be as natural, we probably need to speak out loud.

Praying aloud also helps concentration. Wandering thoughts are much more likely to come if we engage in mental prayer rather than audible prayer. My mind is much less easily drawn off from its fellowship with God when I can hear what I'm saying to Him.

No instruction is given in the Bible about posture in prayer, although kneeling, where possible, seems to be the example we find most commonly. But kneeling - especially when we're tired - can sometimes induce sleep. Variation is helpful, and when concentration is difficult, I frequently find walking, and praying aloud are great helps to me.

We learn to pray by praying. We improve our method of praying by using one method and then adapting it or improving it to meet our circumstances and needs. If we're doubtful as to what is best for us, the answer is to ask God for His Spirit's guidance, and, at the same time, to try that which most appeals to us. The Holy Spirit will soon show us the way forward. If we do nothing, we can't expect Him to do anything to help us. But if we try that which seems worthwhile, we can trust Him to confirm its rightness or lead us into something better.

A prayer

Lord, I thank You again for the gift of prayer, and for all Your great promises which encourage me to utilise the privilege. Forgive me where, through my lack of seriousness and my neglect of method, I've not used my privilege. Please show me the pattern that is right for me, and help me to follow it with the assistance of Your gracious Holy Spirit. Keep me from ever making any method an end in itself, and, at the same time, deliver me from failing to achieve what I ought to in prayer because of a neglect of method. Help me to learn to pray by praying. I pray in Jesus' Name. Amen.

6

Praying for others

'I'll be praying for you.' That's a promise which has been made to us many times probably, and a promise we've made to others. The carrying out of the promise is harder than the making of the promise. But performance in this area of prayer is important - we are intended to pray for one another.

There's a necessary balance to be struck between praying for ourselves and praying for others. We may find ourselves becoming selfish in our prayers, concentrating entirely on our own needs and preoccupations. That's an unhealthy position, and we need to correct it whenever we recognise it happening. At the same time it's not inappropriate or out of place to pray for ourselves. Prayer for our own needs is a God-given privilege and an exercise of our soul in which to engage daily. But we should pray *as much* for others as for ourselves. We are taught to love our neighbour *as ourself* (Luke 10: 27). It's good to aim at praying as much for others as for our own interests and, if possible, more so.

Intercession

The word used to describe praying for others is 'intercession'. Paul instructed Timothy, 'I urge, then, first of all, that requests, prayers, *intercession* and thanksgiving be made for everyone... (1 Timothy 2: 1).

To intercede is to approach a person on behalf of someone else. Intercession in prayer is approaching God on behalf of others. We are priests to God, through our Lord Jesus Christ, not only for ourselves but also for others. Intercession is remembering other people and their needs in our prayers (Romans 1: 9), and is a prominent part of prayer in the New Testament (James 5: 16; 2 Thessalonians 3: 1; Ephesians 6: 18, 19).

Abraham

The first example of intercession in the Bible is Abraham's prayer for Sodom and Gomorrah (Genesis 18: 22-23). God shared with Abraham His determination to punish Sodom and Gomorrah on account of their sin, and the outcry of the surrounding people against it (20, 21). No doubt the fact that Abraham's nephew, Lot, for whom he had some family and moral responsibility, lived there, prompted Abraham to pray as he did. No doubt too this was why God chose to let Abraham know what He was about to do. Abraham responded in a most commendable and instructive manner. Three points are worthy of special mention.

The basis of Abraham's intercession was his faith in God's character. 'Far be it from you to do such a thing - to kill the righteous with the wicked, treating the righteous and the wicked alike', Abraham argued, 'Far be it from you! Will not the Judge of all the earth do right?' (Genesis 18: 25).

The truths we know about God's character are the foundation of intercession. In intercession our starting point, as we look at various needs and crises, must not simply be God's promises but what God has revealed about Himself. So, for example, when tragedy occurs, the absolute assurance I have of God's love is the rock upon which I must place my feet and the primary basis of my intercession for others.

Intercession may sometimes appear to be 'haggling' but it may well be a man exploring before God what it's right to ask Him to do. Abraham was in a situation in prayer that he hadn't been in before, and so we're aware, as we read the description of his intercession, that he was feeling his way with a paradoxical mixture of reverence and boldness - a mixture known to all intercessors (Genesis 18: 27).

Abraham's intercession was marked by persistence - the kind of persistence the Lord Jesus commends (Luke 11: 8). Six times Abraham's plea is mentioned in the course of Genesis 18: 22-33. Sure of God's character, we persist in intercession until we know that we've asked for the things which are in accord with God's character, and which will, therefore, glorify Him.

Jesus
Our Lord Jesus Christ set an example of intercession. He prayed for individuals, and an obvious example is Peter. Peter stood out not only as a leader among the apostles but also as the one who blurted out promises to Jesus which he hadn't always thought through. More than all the other disciples, he affirmed his loyalty to Jesus. But Jesus knew that Peter's promises exceeded his strength. Simon Peter's survival, his restoration after failure, and his future usefulness came in answer to Jesus' prayers for him before any of these things took place. 'Simon, Simon,' Jesus said, 'Satan has asked to sift you as wheat. But I have prayed for you, Simon, that your faith may not fail. And when you have turned back, strengthen your brothers' (Luke 22: 31, 32). The Lord Jesus also prayed for His disciples as a group - including His disciples of today - and we find that prayer in John 17. And then, movingly, He prayed for those who put Him to death, 'Father, forgive them, for they do not know what they are doing' (Luke 23: 34).

Paul
The apostle Paul's letters give full proof of his intercession for others. In the course of his letters he writes down the principal benefits which he asks from God for

his readers (Ephesians 1: 15-23; 3: 14-21). Colossians 1: 3-12 is an example of the kind of intercession he made for Christian believers. 'In all my prayers for all of you, I always pray with joy...' is a typical statement (Philippians 1: 4). He prayed specifically for individual Christians like Timothy - 'I constantly remember you in my prayers' (2 Timothy 1: 3). But his intercession wasn't limited to Christian people. Paul prayed for his fellow-countrymen who were without faith in Jesus Christ (Romans 10: 1), and he once interceded for his fellow-passengers on board a ship, and God graciously answered by giving him the personal safety of them all in spite of shipwreck (Acts 27: 24, 44).

Paul's letters also provide evidence of his dependence upon the prayers of others. He didn't hesitate to ask for specific intercession on his own behalf. To the Romans he wrote: 'I urge you, brothers, by our Lord Jesus Christ and by the love of the Spirit, to join me in my struggle by praying to God for me. Pray that I may be rescued from the unbelievers in Judea and that my service in Jerusalem may be acceptable to the saints there, so that by God's will I may come to you with joy and together with you be refreshed' (Romans 15: 30-32). And to the Ephesians he wrote: 'Pray also for me, that whenever I open my mouth, words may be given me so that I will fearlessly make known the mystery of the gospel, for which I am an ambassador in chains. Pray that I may declare it fearlessly, as I should' (Ephesians 6: 19, 20).

Paul's highest commendation of one of his colleagues, Epaphras - who seems to have been the pioneer of the church at Colossae - was that he was 'always wrestling in prayer' for the Colossians that they might 'stand firm in all the will of God, mature and fully assured' (Colossians 4: 12).

The examples of our Lord Jesus Christ, of Abraham and of Paul and his colleague Epaphras are sufficient to confirm beyond doubt the priority of intercession. While we may feel unworthy to pray for ourselves, we have a duty to pray for others. I have to admit that there have been times - fortunately few - when I've just felt unable to ask anything for myself, either because I've been over-whelmed by my own sinfulness or because of circum-stances which have thoroughly perplexed me and I have not known what to ask. But where at all possible such experiences should not stop me praying for others. We may actually sin against God if we don't pray for others - for those with whom God has involved us in the course of our life (1 Samuel 12: 23).

Paul's introduction to his request for the prayers of the Roman Christians gives the clue to two important reasons why we should pray for one another: 'I urge you, brothers, *by our Lord Jesus Christ and by the love of the Spirit,* to join me in my struggle by praying to God for me' (Romans 15: 30). Our Lord Jesus Christ wants us to pray for one another. It is through His sacrifice that we have such free and glorious access to the Father. His express and fore-most command is that we love one another, and when we love one another we pray for one another. When I stop praying for others, my love for them wanes. Secondly, the Holy Spirit puts Christ's love into our hearts for one an-other, and the Holy Spirit both inspires prayer and assists us in it. When our lives are open to the Spirit, and filled by Him, we'll find it a delight to pray for one another. Where there's the fulness of the Spirit, there will be the fulness of love in intercession for one another.

Those for whom we should pray

It's not possible to draw up a definite list of everyone for whom we should pray, but it helps to set down the most obvious. We are told where to start: 'I urge, then,' Paul wrote, 'first of all, that requests, prayers, intercession and thanksgiving be made for everyone - for kings and all those in authority' (1 Timothy 2: 1, 2).

85

Practical Prayer

Those in authority are to have a special place in our prayers, whatever their politics, and whether we agree with them or not. 'The authorities... have been established by God' (Romans 13: 1), and our praying for them arises from this fact, and is strengthened by it. We are also directed as to how we should pray for them: 'that we may live peaceful and quiet lives in all godliness and holiness' (1 Timothy 2: 2). It's right to want peace and security for everyone's benefit, and it's for our own benefit too because they make the fulfilment of our Christian duties easier. By our prayers we may exercise the most powerful influence that exists on a nation's life.

A further reason for praying for those in authority is that 'God our Saviour... wants all men to be saved and to come to a knowledge of the truth' (1 Timothy 2: 3, 4). Leaders of nations are men and women like ourselves, and they share the same need for salvation through Jesus Christ. It's a mistake to leave praying for those in authority to our corporate prayers in public worship. It should be part of our private praying. The radio or television news and daily newspapers can be our prompters. As crises arise, we may cry to God for wisdom to be given to our leaders. As dangerous tendencies show themselves, we may pray for their correction. My personal hunch is that we probably neglect intelligent prayer for governments. Hudson Taylor urged, 'Learn to move man, through God, by prayer alone.'

Those nearest to us have the next claim upon our prayers - parents, children, brothers and sisters, relatives and friends.

Missionaries - and especially those who represent us because they are members of our own Church fellowship - must come high up on our list. We've referred earlier to J O Fraser, a pioneer missionary who worked among the Lisu in China. Even after giving them a written language and translating much of the Scriptures, his converts were few and often unstable. He then wrote to his mother and asked her to call in her Christian neighbours to pray. It was only after this prayer group had begun to function in earnest that 'the break' came in the Lisu tribe.

Our spiritual leaders ought also to be included regularly in our prayers. Privileged as they are, their responsibilities at times may be unenviable. They're often called upon to make decisions, the full reasons for which it may not be right for them to disclose publicly, and for which they may be misunderstood.

Those who are unconverted should be included daily in our intercessions, especially those who belong to our families, our neighbours and friends. In prayer we may pour out our burden for people that they may be saved, as Paul did: 'Brothers, my heart's desire and prayer to God for the Israelites is that they may be saved' (Romans 10: 1). Paul's prayer demonstrates that it's right to pray in general for the salvation of all. Experience proves that God lays a burden upon us for individuals. In praying for the conversion of others, it's always helpful - and part of the intelligent and believing prayer - to pray in accord with what the Scriptures teach about conversion. With this guidance, we pray for the enlightening work of God's Spirit, and then for His convicting and converting work (2 Corinthians 4: 6; John 16: 8-11), causing the individual's heart to be opened to receive the message of the gospel (Acts 16: 14).

Those who are unwell have a claim upon our intercession. Sometimes we don't know how to pray for those who are ill because healing isn't always God's will (2 Corinthians 12: 7-10). On occasions God may give the conviction that it's right to pray specifically for healing, in which case we should respond accordingly. Where He does not, we should pray for God's will to be done, for His strength and courage to be given to the person who is unwell, and for His purposes to be worked out for the individual and for the praise of God's Name.

Those who suffer in any way for the gospel are not to be neglected. 'Remember those in prison', the writer to the Hebrews urges, 'as if you were their fellow prisoners, and those who are ill-treated as if you yourselves were suffering' (Hebrews 13:3). Somewhere in the world at all times there are believers who know persecution and hardship, and are cut off from Christian fellowship. God raises up intercessors for them, and we may be among them.

Our fellow - believers are always to be in our prayers. 'Pray for each other...' James urges (James 5: 16). First of all then, we should pray for those believers with whom we are intimately associated within our church fellowship. This raises the question of how much we should, and how much we do, communicate our personal needs to one another. James has in view the situation where a Christian may be troubled by a particularly strong temptation or evil desire. His own prayers seem weak against it, and so he tells a Christian friend so as to gain the benefit of his prayers. Probably we do this all too little. It's not the kind of thing we should think of doing with many people, and probably it's best done with only one. But ideally we should all have those relationships in the body of Christ where we can share our needs with another believer of the same sex, and pray together, and where we can share his or her needs.

However, intercession for our fellow-believers should go beyond our immediate circle of friends and acquaintances. Our intercession is to be for the whole Church - 'for all the saints' (Ephesians 6: 18). Paul had no direct pastoral or evangelistic responsibility for the Church at

Rome, but having heard of her he prayed for her, and wrote to her (Romans 1:9, 10). We may wonder how well we can pray with intelligence for those we haven't met. The answer is straightforward in that the basic needs of Christians everywhere are the same, and the most helpful intercession is prompted by our understanding of God's Word, and the insight it gives of the common needs of all Christians. Paul hadn't met the Roman Christians, but, knowing the Christian principles of love and concern for one another (Romans 15:1, 2), he knew that it was right to pray for them: 'May the God who gives endurance and encouragement give you a spirit of unity among yourselves as you follow Christ Jesus, so that with one heart and mouth you may glorify the God and Father of our Lord Jesus Christ' (Romans 15:5, 6).

Now there's not a company of Christians anywhere for whom such a prayer isn't relevant. The list we've provided of people for whom we should pray underlines the importance of what we've already established about method, and the value of some form of prayer diary which we could use on a daily basis so as to take intercession seriously.

Follow through a burden

When God stirs up our hearts to pray for someone, it's invariably a sign that He has purposes of blessing for that individual. We can't be sure as to the timing of God's answer, but our duty is to pray, and to pray until we feel the burden lifted, and placed upon the Lord Himself for action. During her youth Isobel Kuhn, who later became a missionary in China, rebelled against the claims of Christ. She went to stay with a Christian family, but she was on the defensive. After a while, she wondered why her hostess hadn't as yet made any effort to get her alone and talk religiously. Little did Isobel Kuhn dream the reason, which she was told only years later. Recalling this period of her life, she wrote:

> 'That first night, after we had all gone to bed, she could not sleep for the burden of *me*. At last she got up and went on her knees asking God the cause. For over an hour she battled in prayer that whatever was the reason He had sent me to them, it might be fulfilled before I left. Not before she felt she had prayed through did she go back to bed' (Isobel Kuhn: *By Searching* (OMF), p 30).

In her helpful book *Affliction*, Edith Schaeffer relates a succession of crises that came to her family all in the space of a few weeks, the climax being a telephone call from the Swiss police about their permission to stay in the country. Now there was a six-hour time difference between Philadelphia and Switzerland, and Edith Schaeffer's mother was fast asleep on the morning when the police rang the Schaeffers' home. She writes:

> 'At three o'clock in the morning, Philadelphia time, my mother awakened from a short but vivid dream. She had dreamt that I had knocked on her door. As she opened it, I tried to speak but could not say a word. She said (when she wrote later to tell me about it) that my face was distressed and my arms were full of heavy packages. She asked, "What is wrong, Edith? Are you in trouble? You look so burdened." And though my mouth seemed to be forming words, I couldn't make a sound. Then she awakened. Being a woman of prayer, she felt that it was not a chance thing that she had awakened, feeling so certain that something was wrong - and she got out of bed to spend the next few hours in prayer. She prayed for whatever the need might be, read her Bible, and then continued praying for our comfort, strength, wisdom, and guidance in our need' (p 174).

Events proved that those prayers were both timely and answered. We may never know the experience of being awakened by a dream, but we'll all know the experience of people being brought to mind during the day or perhaps at moments when we're awake in the night. They should never be passed over. It may be that the more willing we are to respond to such moments the more God gives them to us, since they are a trust.

Intercession at it's best

Thanksgiving is an important part of intercession for others. We see this reflected in all Paul's prayers for his fellow-Christians. Whether writing to an individual like Philemon (Philemon 4) or a group of Christians (1 Thessalonians 1: 2), he expresses his thanksgiving to God for them. God answers prayers of intercession for others, and so whenever we pray again for people there will be benefits already received to be acknowledged. Thanksgiving also causes us to remember good things about people, and what God has done for them, so that we don't pray in a negative way for them, perhaps concentrating on faults we feel need to be corrected.

Sincerity is essential. Prayers from our lips need to be matched by the desires of our hearts (Romans 10: 1). There's danger in simply praying for things without feeling. When we feel that this is happening at all, the answer is not to stop praying, but to pray for sincerity and reality. We may need to pause and ask ourselves, 'For what should I be praying for this person? And what encourages me in God's Word to do so?' We'll often find prayer becoming very much more alive and earnest after doing so. God delights in sincerity, and whenever we're honest with Him about our difficulties in maintaining it, we may be certain of His assistance.

91

Relevance is imperative in intercession. Relevance is achieved by information. To pray with relevance we need to understand the facts of a situation where that's possible. This aspect of intercession applies especially to our praying for missionaries and work overseas. We may gain information from books, from letters, from missionary societies' magazines and newspapers. The latter deserves emphasis because a day won't go by when some item of news doesn't relate either directly or indirectly to the countries in which our missionary representatives work, and it's information that will take several weeks or months to reach us through a missionary society's magazine or a prayer letter. Newspapers, reporting, as they do, news from all over the world, remind us of the responsibility we have of praying intelligently for the governments of other nations, and especially those where our missionaries work, for their work requires the permission and cooperation of governments. Our relevance will be sharpened by the guidance the New Testament letters give as to the kinds of petitions we should bring to God on behalf of missionaries:

1) Deliverance from malicious unbelievers (Romans 15: 30, 31).
2) Acceptance with God's people (2 Corinthians 1: 11; Romans 15: 31).
3) Health of mind and body (Romans 15: 32; 2 Corinthians 1: 8-11).
4) The ability to speak the right words boldly at the opportune moment (Ephesians 6: 19).
5) The turning of difficult circumstances to spiritual good (Philippians 1: 19).
6) The provision of God-given opportunities for preaching Christ (Colossians 4: 3).
7) Progress in the establishment of the Church through the Word (2 Thessalonians 3: 1).

Praying for others

Relevance in prayer increases when we're *as specific as possible* in our requests. Sometimes 'Lord, bless John...' may be all we can pray because of ignorance of his situation. But if such a prayer springs from laziness on our part to think what his needs are or indifference to discovering them, then we're not really praying at all. Generalities kill the reality of intercession. Sometimes we may have to lay a need before God without knowing what to ask, but at least we're being specific about the need. When the wine ran out at the wedding in Cana of Galilee, Mary said, 'They have no more wine' (John 2: 3). She doesn't seem to have known what she should have asked or expected, but she was specific in declaring the need. The centurion did the same in the Gospels, 'Lord', he said to Jesus, 'my servant lies at home paralysed, and in terrible suffering' (Matthew 8: 6). Specific intercession is vital. Having written, 'Pray for us...' the writer to the Hebrews goes on, 'I particularly urge you to pray so that I may be restored to you soon' (Hebrews 13: 18, 19). As the sharpening of a knife makes it more effective, so the endeavour to be specific sharpens prayer and makes it more powerful.

Imagination also has an important role to play as we pray for others. The writer to the Hebrews urges, 'Remember those in prison *as if you were their fellow prisoners* , and those who are ill-treated *as if yourselves were suffering* (13: 3). There's an important key to effective intercession here. Having established the particular responsibility we have for our missionary representatives, the way we fulfil it in prayer is to use our imagination. Put yourself in the place of someone in their first term of service, struggling to learn an unfamiliar language, and having to worship on a Sunday in a language which they don't really understand. Now when we use our imagination like that we begin to pray intelligently and specifically for our friend: for patience, endurance, stickability, deliverance from despondency and a retentive memory. Think too of what it must be like living in a different culture, with new customs, a draining climate and the inevitable tensions of both emotional and physical tiredness. Relationships can become fragile on account of tiredness and the pressures of living in a close community. There are often tensions in our own homes, and how much more so in a closely knit community. As we put ourselves imaginatively in this situation, we pray that our friends may sleep well, that they won't allow little things to become big things, that they will love one another, that they will be helped to laugh at things that might otherwise give rise to an explosion of feeling, and that they may be able to shrug off tendencies to self-pity.

What a difference it makes to our praying for those imprisoned for the gospel, or those who are ill-treated, or those who suffer physical pain, when we try to imagine what it must be like, and then pray accordingly. The Gospels tell the story of the Canaanite woman whose daughter was suffering terribly. When she knelt before Jesus, she cried, 'Lord, help *me* !' (Matthew 15: 25). Intercession means becoming so involved in other people's needs that we are saying, 'Lord, help *me* !' although in fact the prayer is, '*Lord, help them* !'.

Persistence in intercession is essential. Praying for ourselves in fits and starts is foolish; to pray for others in fits and starts is irresponsible. To be faithful in intercession we must remember people 'night and day' (2 Timothy 1: 3) with constancy (Romans 1: 9). We show the importance we attach to intercession by the time we give to it. The Lord Jesus taught that we 'should always pray and not give up' (Luke 18: 1).

The power of intercessory prayer isn't to be underestimated. 'The prayer of a righteous man is powerful and effective' (James 5: 16). It's not a matter of its *perhaps* being effective, *it is* . Prayer may anticipate need so that as we pray for someone serving God overseas, God in His mercy may be anticipating his or her needs. Sometimes prayer may even follow need and still be effective because God answers before we call. He knew we were going to pray - He still requires us to call. Prayer can jump every hurdle and overcome all obstacles. If we wanted to get in touch with friends at a distance this moment, we might find it difficult - there might be a delay in communications or they might be inaccessible. But with no delay, we may come into God's presence, in the name of the Lord Jesus, assured of the power and authority of His Name, and obtain the power and grace of God on behalf of our friends. Intercession and the help of God's Spirit are vitally linked, and are the way God's deliverance comes (Philippians 1: 19). We help one another by our prayers (2 Corinthians 1: 11), joining in one another's struggles and battles (Romans 15: 30).

Intercession is a two-way exercise: we pray for others and others pray for us. George Whitefield was on board a ship bound for America, and he wrote in his diary: 'Was enlarged in intercession, and had reason to believe there was sweet communion kept up between us and our friends on shore. The assurance of their prayers often lifts up my hands when they hang down, and strengthens my feeble knees'.

Speaking of giving, our Lord Jesus declared, 'Give, and it will be given to you. A good measure, pressed down, shaken together and running over, will be poured into your lap. For with the measure you use, it will be measured to you' (Luke 6: 38). I've a strong suspicion that the principle applies to praying for others too. Those who give themselves to secret intercession for others may find themselves at the receiving end of the prayers of others more than they will ever know this side of heaven.

A prayer

Heavenly Father, I thank You for all whom You have prompted over the years to pray for me. I'm grateful for those who pray for me today. In Your love and kindness meet their needs as You do mine.

I want to take seriously my privilege and responsibility to pray for others. Make me sensitive to any burden You wish to place upon me. Stir me whenever I become lethargic or lazy in intercession. Strengthen me in my desire to pray earnestly, relevantly and persistently. Stir up my imagination to understand the needs of those in totally different situations from my own, so that I pray with sympathy and feeling. May I not sin against You by failing to pray for anyone You want me to bring to You. For Jesus Christ's sake. Amen.

7

Praying with others

Every Christian worthy of the name wants the Church of Jesus Christ to be kept in good health and to grow. Praying together - what we term 'corporate prayer' - stands out as one of the basic secrets of the Church's spiritual health and growth. Martin Luther wrote: 'Let us pray in the Church with the Church for the Church, for there are three things that preserve the Church and belong to the Church. First, to teach faithfully; then, to pray diligently; and third, to suffer with earnestness.'

Prayer with others constitutes a lovely privilege as members of God's spiritual family. When a human family comes together, its members enjoy not only talking to their brothers and sisters but also to their parents. In God's spiritual family, we enjoy talking and sharing with one another - that's an essential feature of belonging to the Christian family - but, in particular, we enjoy talking together to our heavenly Father. Of course, we can talk to Him on our own, but there's special profit and pleasure in coming together, as brothers and sisters to the same Father.

Praying with others may be quite strange and foreign at first - and even off-putting. Temperament inevitably enters into it, and if we're naturally shy we may be inclined to shirk participating audibly in a Church prayer meeting, or when a group of Christians with whom we are meeting suggest praying for matters of common concern. If we don't overcome our hesitancy, non-participation may become a habit - and even a life-long practice, detrimental to ourselves and others. I'm grateful that after the first prayer meeting I ever went to, an elderly lady next to me asked,'Why didn't you pray?' Her question shook me somewhat! At the next prayer meeting, through her encouragement I prayed, and began the establishment of life-long habit of never going to a prayer meeting without expecting to take part. William Cowper, the hymn writer, was very diffident about praying publicly, until John Newton, his minister, helped him to overcome his diffidence, and then his voice was heard regularly. Perhaps some require similar encouragement, and others need to provide that kind of encouragement to other Christians. Habit has more to do with the development of our spiritual life and activity than we sometimes credit.

Promises and practice

Corporate prayer has promises attached to it by God that underline its importance. God promises in the Old Testament, 'if my people, who are called by my name, will humble themselves and pray and seek my face and turn from their wicked ways, then will I hear from heaven and will forgive their sin and will heal their land' (2 Chronicles 7: 14). In the New Testament the Lord Jesus promises, 'if two of you on earth agree about anything you ask for, it will be done for you by my Father in heaven. For where two or three come together in my name, there am I with them' (Matthew 18: 19, 20). God commits Himself to dealing with His people's needs in answer to corporate prayer.

Many promises regarding prayer - commonly applied primarily to ourselves as individuals - are promises made in the first instance to the local Church as a whole. We tend - perhaps inevitably - to read the Bible in an individualistic or personal way, applying everything first of all to ourselves. But the New Testament letters were mainly letters to Churches, and when promises about prayer were given, the first readers and hearers would have recognised them as applying as much to their praying together as to their personal prayers. Corporate prayer finds encouragement in the Lord's Prayer in that we are taught to pray 'Our Father' and not simply 'My Father'.

The early Church practised corporate prayer as part of the essence of its life. The early Church was born in a prayer meeting. Following the Lord's ascension, the disciples waited in Jerusalem as He had instructed. We don't read of any specific instruction from our Lord that they should spend the time in prayer, but they knew enough from all He had taught them in His three years of ministry that it was the right use of their time. 'They all joined together constantly in prayer' and 'When the day of Pentecost came, they were all together in one place' (Acts 1: 14; 2: 1), and the Spirit came upon them in dramatic power. Joining together for prayer became one of the immediate marks of the Church's life, in that together with the apostles' teaching, fellowship, and the breaking of bread, they 'devoted themselves... to prayer' (Acts 2: 42). They continued as they had begun. There's no doubt that this had much to do with their experience of the Lord adding 'to their number daily those who were being saved' (Acts 2: 47). The power of the Holy Spirit was released as the early Church used the weapon of corporate prayer.

One of the characteristics of the early Christians which is often missing in contemporary Christianity is boldness. The early Christians weren't on the defensive but were on the offensive in their witness to Jesus. They shared the same natural reluctance we all have to stand out and to be different in the world. But they discovered that the secret of boldness and success came through prayer. When Peter and John were told not to preach any more in Jesus' name, the Church's immediate reaction was to raise their voices together in prayer to God, and 'After they prayed, the place where they were meeting was shaken. And they were all filled with the Holy Spirit and spoke the word of God boldly' (Acts 4: 31). It's not more committee meetings on evangelism that are needed, but prayer meetings followed by immediate engagement in evangelism. A church with a strong prayer meeting is a church with a strong witness. The people who know how to humble themselves before God are bold before men and women in the preaching of the good news of Jesus.

God's guidance came to the early Church as it waited upon God in prayer and worship. The Church at Antioch knew it had responsibility for the vast Gentile world. They honestly faced up to Jesus' last commission to preach the gospel to all creation. It was while they were worshipping the Lord and fasting - both activities are associated with prayer - that the Holy Spirit directed them to Paul and Barnabas as the right men to send. 'So after they had fasted and prayed, they placed their hands on them and sent them off' (Acts 13:3). Corporate prayer is the proper context and atmosphere for Church decisions - that doesn't preclude discussion and debate, but it saves them from being unprofitable. God promises wisdom in answer to prayer (James 1: 5), and that promise has just as much a church application as a personal application.

Deliverance came to Christians - both for themselves and to others - as they prayed together. The early Church hit a crisis point when the apostle Peter was wrongly imprisoned by King Herod and threatened with execution. Luke's immediate comment is instructive: 'So Peter was kept in prison, but the church was earnestly praying to God for him' (Acts 12: 5). On the night he was miraculously released from prison by God, Peter knew where he would find Christians, for he went to Mary's house 'where many people had gathered and were praying' (Acts 12: 12). Later, Paul and Silas were imprisoned in a Philippian gaol, cut off from their fellow-believers. But only two people were required for corporate prayer, and 'About midnight Paul and Silas were praying...' and God's deliverance came (Acts 16: 25). Corporate prayer is the Church's secret of seeing God doing what seems impossible. Corporate prayer remains the way to deal with difficulties and pressures, as many parts of the tested and persecuted body of Christ testify. Christians in Barnaul, Siberia, have had to fight in recent years for their lives and their faith. How have they survived?

'We learned to depend strongly on prayer. At every meeting we prayed, and on Wednesday night we met specifically to pray,' one of the deacons recalls. 'During times of trouble we placed extra emphasis on prayer. For example, once when one of our members was arrested, we determined to pray for him at Church every three hours. Wherever we went - at work or at school - we prayed silently in the Spirit. It seemed to us that no one in the world knew or cared about our problems but God. We decided we must turn to Him every three hours to find comfort, strength and direction.

'Our Church in Barnaul and Churches all over Russia decided to designate every Friday as a day of prayer and fasting. We were comforted to know that on that day the sacrifice of prayer and praise was being offered to the God of heaven from every corner of our atheistic country.' (Anita and Peter Deyneka: *A Song in Siberia* p 58.)

The first recourse

Corporate prayer should be the automatic response of God's people to situations which are beyond them to cope with, and which threaten the progress of the gospel and the honour of God's Name in the world.

Prayer is the most vital weapon in the spiritual battle in which we're continually involved (Ephesians 6: 10ff). When we become aware of Satan's attacks on the personal level, that's a call to personal prayer. When we feel the reality of Satan's onslaughts on us as a body of believers that's a call to the employment and maintenance of corporate prayer.

Many matters which so easily become merely subjects for gossip ought instead to be subjects for prayer. Gossip leads to disaster; prayer leads to victory. God's promise of peace, as a consequence of praying about everything, isn't a promise simply to the Christian as a private individual - it's a promise made to the local Church (Philippians 4: 6, 7). There are always many issues which can disturb the Church's peace - our spiritual adversary sees to that. It's never God's will that His peace should be absent from the Church, and corporate prayer is the means God has provided to make that peace the Church's regular experience.

The sense of family

A healthy family accepts both its joys and responsibilities. It's good to belong, and it's right to help one another. To belong to God's family brings tremendous joy most of the time. I deliberately say 'most of the time' since membership of God's family, like membership of a human family, produces its own difficulties and heartaches as we have to face disappointments on account of human frailty. Members of a healthy family unit rally to one another's assistance when need arises. Basic to all the help we can give one another is our praying for one another. A Church prayer meeting is often the only way to get to know the needs of other members of God's local family who are not our immediate friends or acquaintances.

I've often been thrilled to hear a Christian pray with understanding and feeling for one of our missionaries overseas or for someone ill in hospital as I've realised that he or she has never met the person for whom he or she is praying. In the Church prayer meeting we learn to bear one another's burdens. Christians who neglect corporate prayer are like soldiers who leave their front-line comrades in the lurch. Corporate prayer is a form of Christian cooperation (2 Corinthians 1: 11). There's time both to give to others by corporate prayer and to receive from them. Most of us would want our fellow Christians to pray for us, if for example, we were ill in hospital. We would expect to be mentioned in the Church prayer meeting. When we're better we have a duty to repay our debt by being at the prayer meeting, when possible, to pray for others who, having prayed for us, are now themselves in the position we were once in.

It would be a fascinating exercise to trace the unique place corporate prayer has had in the progress and history of the Church. Jonathan Edwards, the New England eighteenth-century theologian, wrote, 'When God is about to do a great work, He pours out a spirit of supplication'. He had personal experience of spiritual revival among the people of God, and his words are worth noting and taking to heart.

A particular discipline

To share in prayer with others - whether in an informal group or in a more formal Church prayer meeting - requires a particular discipline. On a cold winter's night the comfort of an armchair in front of the fire may be much more attractive than venturing out to a prayer meeting. But if we make it our habit to be present whenever possible, then we'll achieve that discipline. We mentioned earlier William Cowper's connection with the Church of which John Newton was pastor. The Church at Olney had a prayer meeting in what was known as 'the Great House' on Sunday mornings at 6 am. William Cowper went regularly, and he describes it:

'On Sabbath mornings in winter I rose before day and... trudged... often through snow and rain to a prayer meeting at the Great House... There I always found forty or fifty poor folks who preferred a glimpse of the light of God's countenance and favour to the

comforts of a warm bed, or to any comforts that the
world could afford them and there I have often myself
partaken that blessing with them.'

There's a discipline too in preparing ourselves for
sharing in corporate prayer. This above any other factor
may determine the success of our prayers. The effectiveness of any prayer meeting is intimately related to the
spiritual health of those who take part. Paul's instruction
to Timothy provides a clue to the preparation that's necessary: 'I want men everywhere to lift up holy hands in
prayer, without anger or disputing' (1 Timothy 2: 8).
Three things receive specific mention: holiness, anger
and disputing (or resentment). One of the requirements
has reference to our relationship to God, and the other
two to our relationships with others.

Our lives must be in harmony with God's holiness as
we pray together. We can't live a day without facing
temptation and finding sin a peril. Our hearts are quickly
attracted to the things of this present world rather than of
the world to come. We easily become self-centred rather
than God-centred in our thoughts. As we ask for God's
help, His Spirit will help us in the confession of our sins so
that we enter into a prayer meeting cleansed and walking
'in the light, as he is in the light' (1 John 1: 7).

At the same time we must make sure that there's no
anger or resentment in our feelings or attitudes to others.
If we're not in a right relationship with our fellow-Christians, we'll either not want to pray for them, or we'll do so
hypocritically. It's easy enough to feel hurt at times and to
bear resentment, but to remain hurt and resentful is always contrary to God's will, no matter what excuses we
may make. If we're refusing to forgive anyone what he or
she has done to us, then God will withhold His forgiveness, much as Satan may try to suggest to the contrary.
Our reluctance to meet together for prayer may stem
sometimes from our neglect of holiness and a sense of

estrangement from other Christians. The neglect of private prayer soon leads to neglect of corporate prayer. If I lose my desire to join in prayer with others, I urgently need to ask myself the question, 'Why?' because it's always a danger sign.

Practicalities

We need to be disciplined as we take part audibly in corporate prayer. Basic to the expression of Christian love is the desire to do good to others and to be helpful to them. It's possible to take part in a prayer meeting, or a prayer group, unhelpfully. Although it may seem to be stating the obvious, let's spell out some of the basics.

Pray naturally
Probably we've all heard people pray in a manner entirely different from the way in which they normally speak. It may be they are copying others, or perhaps they feel that it's rather spiritual to have a particular tone of voice. Be yourself as you lead others in prayer. Because the person who has prayed before you has appeared particularly fervent, don't feel that your tone has to be the same. Fervency isn't so much a matter of tone of voice but of spirit and heart - and God looks upon the latter.

Pray where possible with a particular Scripture, or the general teaching of Scripture, in mind
Leading others in prayer demands agreement on their part, and their minds must be exercised to test whether the request to which their agreement is sought is in accord with God's will. When Scripture is properly used to guide prayers, agreement comes about quickly and naturally. As subjects and topics for prayer are raised, think of where in God's Word you gain direction as to how to pray for such a need or situation. Turn that guidance from the Scriptures into believing prayer.

Pray simply and directly

I hope you won't misunderstand me when I say that it's possible to pray publicly with a lot of padding and sheer wordiness. We can get into the habit of always using the same words so that in the end we're not really thinking what we are praying. Something which helps to correct this, and which adds life and vitality to a prayer meeting, is the habit of usually praying for only one thing at a time, and doing so quickly - that is to say, getting immediately to the point!

Pray briefly

This is perhaps the single most important direction. It's not a mark of spirituality to pray long prayers. While long prayers are permissible they aren't the most beneficial prayers in a prayer meeting. Long prayers are less inclined to be specific than short prayers. John McNeill, a Scottish evangelist, was at a prayer meeting before one of his evangelistic services. A saintly old man prayed at great length, ranging over a wide field. Mr McNeill was obviously very uncomfortable, but sat with bowed head and held himself in check. When a member of the committee complained afterwards, John McNeill who had a good sense of humour, remarked, 'Oh, aye, it was one of thae guid soond auld-fashioned prayers that the angels ken sae weel; and they just pop it into a pigeon-hole, saying "Aye, that'll dae ony time".'

The tax-collector in the story Jesus told, prayed simply, 'God, have mercy on me, a sinner' (Luke 18: 13), a proof that the shortest of prayers can express the most sincere desire and bring the most amazing answer. George Whitefield once rebuked a man who prayed too long by saying, 'Sir, you prayed me into a good frame, and then you prayed me out of it.' John Newton wrote, 'it is better... that the hearers should wish the prayer had been longer, than spend half or a considerable part of the time in wishing it was over'. A prayer meeting with many people contributing by means of brief specific prayers tends to be a much more effective prayer meeting than one where only a few take part praying long prayers.

If ever we find ourselves concluding that it's only a small number of people who pray - and perhaps the same people - and we feel this in a critical manner, then we have the answer open to us, and a most beneficial and constructive one - to determine whenever possible to take part ourselves, even in the briefest of petitions or expressions of praise. Another benefit of shorter prayers as the norm is that we're then less inclined to be led astray by natural eloquence or the pride which may come if people foolishly begin to express their admiration of the manner in which we pray.

Pray audibly
This obvious part is easily overlooked. Some of us have soft voices compared with the loud and strong voices of others. If your voice is soft, then you'll need to be sensible as to where in the room you sit and how you pray aloud. Sit in the centre of the meeting place rather than at its circumference. If possible, stand up to pray, and if you don't stand make sure you don't bury your face in your hands so that your voice is lost. It's an embarrassment if a young person with a soft voice prays at the same time as an older person who is becoming deaf! But both have a place in the prayer meeting, and the embarrassment can be avoided with a little common sense and concern for one another.

It's not unspiritual to have these practical guidelines for taking part in a prayer meeting or in corporate prayer. It's because we believe it to be such an important part of the Spirit's work in our personal life and in our corporate life that we feel it worthy of our best effort and concern. The Holy Spirit's presence and guidance are the most important factors in a prayer meeting. But often when people ignore these practical guidelines, what they may describe as 'the Spirit's freedom' may not really be such at all, but rather human frailty. The Holy Spirit doesn't delight in order for order's sake, but He does delight in business-like prayer which arises from faith and the determination to take God at His Word, and to honour Him in the most practical ways.

But we mustn't overemphasise audible participation in corporate prayer, and so get it out of perspective. Not everyone who comes to a prayer meeting will take part audibly - and often there won't be an opportunity to do so - but that doesn't make an individual's contribution any the less. One person leads in prayer in order that the prayer of one might become the prayer of all. I may participate to the full in a prayer meeting by joining my silent prayers with the audible prayers of others. The essential contribution I must aim at is agreement (Matthew 18: 19). As one and another pray, I must be testing my own convictions and understanding of God's will so that I may add my positive agreement to that prayer, and if I do agree than I have the privilege of adding my 'Amen' at the conclusion of the prayer. Baby-sitting one evening a grandmother put her granddaughter to bed. 'Let's pray together,' she suggested. 'You pray first,' the three-year-old replied. Grandma prayed, and then waited for her granddaughter. 'Aren't you going to pray?' she asked after a rather long pause. 'I did pray,' her granddaughter replied, 'I said "Amen" after you had prayed.' The little girl had grasped a truth adults often miss. The Bible tells us that the 'Amen' is to be said - not whispered or taken for granted (Psalm 106: 48). Aim at saying, 'Amen' loud enough for your neighbour on either side to hear.

Encouragements

There are valuable 'spin-offs' from praying together which encourage us all the more to make proper use of it. It's a general principle of life that unity brings strength, and it applies to prayer. Next to sharing in the Lord's Supper, corporate prayer is where we sense and express our oneness in our Lord Jesus Christ the most. We feel each other's burdens and share them as we identify with the feelings and convictions of the one who prays or the person for whom prayer is offered.

Corporate prayer has a warming influence upon the soul, and stimulates faith. 'As iron sharpens iron, so one man sharpens another' (Proverbs 27: 17). We may come together not much inclined to pray at first, but the prayer of another Christian soon warms our soul and stirs up our faith to expect much of God. We may come to a prayer meeting with a conviction of sorts about a matter, but not a sure conviction. Then, to our amazement, we discover through the prayer of someone else that he or she shares the same conviction, and our own conviction is clarified and strengthened, and turned into believing prayer. God may choose to reveal and confirm His will in some personal and private matter through the prayers of others without their knowing anything about it. I've found this happening frequently. Just this past week I was in a Church vestry before a Church Anniversary service in a Church different from the one to which I belong. I was concerned to know that the message I had prepared was the right one. Imagine my joy and assurance when someone in the prayer meeting beforehand prayed using the actual words of Scripture I was going to share with the congregation.

Some of the best learning is often unconscious learning, and we learn to pray through listening to and joining in the prayers of others who are further on in God's school of prayer than we are. We also get to know and love our fellow-Christians, both old and young, through praying together. There are Christians with whom I've never had the opportunity of sitting down and chatting but whom I feel I really know because of their prayers. The fellowship of corporate prayer is a most precious privilege, and

the Christian who deprives himself of it deprives himself
of one of God's superlative encouragements and blessings.

A prayer

*Thank You, Father, for Your family, and for every op-
portunity of coming to You in united prayer. Forgive me
where I've neglected or taken for granted such opportunities. Pardon me where I've been critical of other
people's prayers, and haven't made any effort to participate myself.*

*I want to identify with Your people in prayer, and to
bear and share others' burdens. May Your Spirit help me
to enter into the prayers of others, so that by Your Spirit I
may add my 'Amen', making their prayers as much mine
as theirs. I ask especially that my habits in corporate
prayer may be good ones, and that I may be sensitive to
anything You want to teach me. May I play my part in
Your people's work through prayer, with the joy that
comes from obedient faith. For Jesus' sake. Amen.*

8

Problems and questions about prayer

I've found myself a little hesitant in using the word 'problems' since it can lead to merely negative thinking. Nevertheless we do encounter problems of understanding in that we know that we can't use this privilege properly without knowing exactly how God wants us to think of it. Others are problems of practice that we have to find time and opportunity to pray, and when we do so we want to make certain that our prayers are effective and pleasing to God.

So as to be sure that I deal with the most pressing problems and questions about prayer, I asked three separate groups of people to share with me honestly their problems and questions. The identical nature of the majority of them makes me feel that they are probably the principal ones. It would be a gross presumption on my part to think that in one brief chapter I can begin to answer all or any of the questions adequately. What I propose to do is to provide 'starters' which you can think through yourself. As the questions frequently overlap so too must the answers.

'What should I do with the feelings of inadequacy I sometimes feel when I begin to pray? And also what about my feelings of unworthiness?'

You're not unique in these feelings. The more we grasp the immensity of our privilege in prayer, the more we feel inadequate. If we don't then perhaps there's something wrong in our appreciation of prayer.

Remember that it's 'by the blood of Jesus, by a new and living way opened for us' (Hebrews 10: 19, 20), that

111

we're able to approach God. It's because we are inadequate of ourselves that God has taken so much trouble to make prayer simple and basic. It's not our adequacy that matters but our Father's desire to meet us as we pray in the Name of His Son. Whatever may be the reasons for our feelings of inadequacy, our Lord Jesus' atoning death on the Cross deals with every obstacle.

Remember that it's to your heavenly Father that you come. He delights in your coming to Him. His love for you exceeds all you could ever ask or think. Remember that at your Father's right hand there's your Saviour, your great High Priest (Hebrews 10: 21), whose finished work guarantees your acceptance with God, and He perfectly understands your every feeling. Remember that within you there's the Holy Spirit who intercedes for you with groanings that words can't express. He's immediately aware of your feelings of inadequacy, and He's there to help you turn them into effective prayer for strength. I've deliberately used the word 'remember' a number of times because when I'm tempted to be guided by my feelings - or sometimes my lack of feelings - I need to be guided by what I've already been taught by God.

A feeling of unworthiness is also not unusual. We're not worthy, and never will be. None of us is worthy. It's because we are unworthy that the Lord Jesus died and made this way of access for us into God's presence. What matters is not our adequacy and worthiness but the worthiness of Jesus Christ before God, and the adequacy of His finished work upon the Cross. Jesus Himself is our worthiness, since God the Father reckons Jesus' righteousness to us through faith.

It's appropriate that we should be aware of our unworthiness, but never to the point where it stops us praying. If it does, then the enemy of our souls has led us to an extreme which God never intends. Sometimes our renewed sense of unworthiness may be because we've fallen into sin. The right thing then is to confess that sin honestly and to trust God for His gracious forgiveness.

Where should I begin learning how to pray?'

We can't do better than to follow the disciples' example when they said to Jesus, 'Lord, teach us to pray' (Luke 11:1). We should ask God Himself to teach us to pray, and how to pray.

The answer our Lord gave the disciples was to teach them what we commonly know as 'the Lord's Prayer'. We won't go far wrong in using it both as a prayer and employing it as a guide to the priorities we should follow in prayer. In addition, it's helpful to use the many prayers found in the book of Psalms, together with the prayers that are scattered throughout the New Testament. Whenever you come across one in your daily reading of the Bible, make a note of it and either turn it into a prayer for yourself and others, or use it as a further guide to the kind of prayers that please God.

Learn to pray by joining in prayers with others. Looking back, I realise that I've gained more than I can calculate through hearing the prayers of others, and especially the prayers of more mature Christians. A young child learns to talk by listening to the words and conversations of its elders, and that's one of the basic ways in which we learn to pray.

Never forget too that the Holy Spirit lives within you, and He's always present to assist you as you pray. Like most things in life, we learn most by doing the thing we want to learn. We won't learn to pray by listening to sermons or reading books unless at the same time we actually pray. We learn to pray by praying - so pray!

'What should I do when I don't feel like praying?'

Once again we're not unique in this. The most important thing is to be honest about it, and not just allow ourselves to 'go through the motions' of prayer without meaning anything we say. And by being honest about it, I mean being honest with God too. Confess to Him reverently and contritely that you don't feel like praying, and ask Him to help you by His Spirit as you quietly wait before Him.

At the same time - as you wait quietly before God in an attitude of prayer, without saying anything - see if any reason comes to mind which might account for your feeling that you don't want to pray or can't pray. It may be that failure or sin has not been confessed or that you are in some way double-minded in your praying (James 1: 8), perhaps without having realised it. On the other hand you may recognise that there's a straightforward and perfectly understandable physical cause for your not feeling like prayer. Once you discern the cause do something about it. If it's unconfessed sin or double-mindedness, confess the truth to God and ask for forgiveness. If the cause is physical, don't be hard on yourself, but cast yourself upon God's mercy for His special assistance, remembering that He - more than anyone - knows your weakness and is sympathetic towards you in it.

Sometimes there may be no discernible reason, and the process of self-examination, having yielded nothing, may prompt discouragement. While on the one hand we can't simply pray to order, there are things, nevertheless, we can do to help ourselves. Just to give up praying is always dangerous. Somehow or other we need to get the soul's machinery turning over, rather like the engine of a car in cold weather. I've found a number of practices useful, such as praying aloud one of the Psalms or one of Paul's prayers in his New Testament letters. I sometimes reach for my hymn book and read through - or even sing to myself - one of the hymns which directs my attention to the Lord Himself. I also find it helpful to always have on the go either a Christian biography or a Christian classic which I can take up when for any reason I feel spiritually sluggish, and especially in prayer. One or other of these means always proves effective.

'What should I do when I feel that I'm getting nowhere in my prayers?'

I'm inclined to want to ask, 'How do you know that you're getting nowhere in your prayers?' since such a question may arise from a mistaken assessment of our situation. God does hear my prayers whether I'm aware of it or not. But behind the question there may be the feeling that our prayers somehow or other don't get beyond the ceiling - we don't feel we are getting through to God. The situation isn't dissimilar to our previous question. The first thing to do is to ask yourself if there's any reason why prayer might be difficult. The answer may be unconfessed sin (Psalm 66: 18). A common cause is lack of genuine submission to God, seen sometimes in our holding back from praying about a certain subject because we aren't sure that we'll either be happy with, or will accept, God's answer. Or it may be that we've approached prayer in a manner which isn't pleasing to God, and He wants to bring us up with some kind of a jolt to show us what's right. If, as we examine ourselves, the cause becomes apparent, deal with it honestly; and if no cause becomes obvious, cry to God for assistance.

'What should I do when I don't know what to pray for?'

This question doesn't have regard to the general requests we know we should always be making - such as those the Lord's Prayer brings before us - but how we should pray on those occasions when we know prayer is essential and when we feel that prayer needs to be specific. An example that will register immediately is serious illness. Should we automatically pray for healing? We know that prayer is appropriate but how should we pray?

It's always right to begin with honesty. If you don't have any conviction as to how you should pray, tell God so, and ask Him to guide you as you think through how you should approach Him on behalf of the person who's ill.

Turn over in your mind Scriptures which have some bearing on the subject. Then apply those Scriptures in your prayers to your friend's need. It may still be that you can't pray specifically for healing, but as you affirm your confidence in God's perfect love and wisdom, you can pray from your heart that God's will may be done in your friend's life even as it's done in heaven.

There will be occasions when we don't know what to pray for because we're totally overwhelmed by sorrow and distress. We must never forget the power of the little word 'Father'. When a young child cries out in the middle of the night 'Daddy!' or 'Mummy!' - not always knowing what's wrong, and what it needs - the cry itself will bring forth the appropriate response on the part of the caring parent. When we cry from our hearts, 'Father', our heavenly Father marshals all the resources of heaven to aid us, because He perfectly reads all the need that lies behind our cry.

How may I avoid getting into a rut in the way in which I pray? How can I avoid vain repetition?'

To be asking such questions is healthy because if we're not sensitive to these problems we're more than likely to fall into them. There's no single answer, but a number of suggestions may be made which go some way towards dealing with the problems.

First, deliberately respond in prayer to God as you read the Scriptures each day, taking up the words of Scripture where possible, turning them into prayer. This morning I read in Exodus 34: 29 and 35 of Moses' face becoming radiant as a result of his conversations with the Lord. Psalm 34: 5 came to mind, and I prayed that as I look to the Lord I might also display the radiance of faith. I may have prayed that prayer before, but certainly not for a long while. As I allow my reading of the Bible to guide many of my daily prayers, variety is present, and that avoids the rut of always asking for the same things, and sometimes without the proper thought that prayer deserves.

Second, pray with some personal method or programme, but ensure that your method includes variation and that on certain days you alter the order so that every day isn't the same. If you feel that you're getting into a rut - as I sometimes do - even in the use of the varied pattern you try to follow, abandon your usual method for a day. I find it helpful to do this once a week, usually on my day off. It's also sometimes extremely refreshing and effective to pray more slowly than usual, so as to avoid familiar phrases and perhaps cliches. Normally when we pray, we should just let our mouth express what our heart feels - and automatically we'll employ well-used phrases and words with real meaning and intention. But to stop once in a while so as to choose our words deliberately avoids rut-making.

A further help is to include in your method of prayer the occasional or regular practice of beginning your time of prayer with a period of meditation on different aspects of God's character. This exercise needs to be unhurried. Rather than feeling that I must immediately say something to God when I come into His presence, in meditation I simply try to think about Him - using the Bible to help me - until I can keep quiet no longer and am compelled to praise and thank Him, and cry to Him for His blessing.

Jesus warned against the danger of empty repetition: 'And when you pray, do not keep on babbling like pagans, for they think they will be heard because of their many words. Do not be like them, for your Father knows what you need before you ask him' (Matthew 6: 7, 8). If you feel you're getting into a habit of empty repetition, deliberately pause before you pray, and say to yourself, 'God helping me, I'm only going to say what I mean, and I'm going to pray thoughtfully, whether my prayers are long or short.'

'How can I fit in sufficient time for prayer in the busyness of life? And how do I know if I've spent enough time in prayer?'

It's always a battle to fit in sufficient time for prayer - the enemy of our souls sees to that. It's impossible to say what a 'sufficient' time for prayer is for anyone else, or even for oneself. It may not be the right question to ask since it tends to place the emphasis upon quantity rather than quality. There's something wrong in any relationship when one of the parties has his or her eye on the clock. When a husband and wife enjoy spending time together, they wouldn't say that it should be thirty minutes or two hours, but simply that they enjoy being together, whether it's for a short or long period. And so it is in our fellowship with God.

Our situations vary tremendously, and God is intimately acquainted with our personal circumstances. What may be sufficient time for a young mother with young children to look after may be totally insufficient time for someone with no family responsibilities. God knows the time we can give Him, and the time we ought to give, and He rewards us with the encouragement our individual circumstances require.

No matter how busy our daily timetable, we do well to establish a set time when we can best be alone with God. Having worked out the most suitable time, we mustn't make that time a rod for our own back by feeling guilty if some particular day we can't manage it. As well as your set time or times, make prayer a continual practice by praying as often as you find someone brought to your mind for prayer or you find yourself in need of direction or assistance. You don't need to close your eyes to pray. If you ask a healthy Christian, 'How many times have you prayed today?' probably he ought to answer, 'I can't tell you - I've prayed so often!'

When Christians are together or perhaps talking over the phone, needs will often be shared. I find it a constant help to pray with them there and then. For one thing this means that you don't have to wait until the end of the day to remember what you should be praying for - and there's also particular power in united prayer.

We've established that it's the quality of our relationship with God that counts rather than the exact number of minutes we spend in prayer. If we have a prayer diary, as we suggested earlier, we'll only feel we've prayed sufficiently each day when we've covered all the needs and people we've written down for that day of the week or the month. Beware of making your prayer list for each day too long because it can become something like a shopping list that you rattle off hurriedly. You may feel reluctant to be selective in your prayers in case someone is not prayed for -especially missionaries. Be selective according to the particular burden you feel. As you ask the Holy Spirit to do this for you, you may be assured that He will be placing burdens for other missionaries upon other Christians. The 'operations room' for prayer isn't open to our scrutiny but it's under the direction of the Holy Spirit.

To know just how much time to spend in prayer for a matter of particular urgency is a pressing question. A crisis arises and we know that we must share it with our heavenly Father. How are we to know when to stop praying? And does there come a point when to pray any more would indicate unbelief? In some situations it's a matter of praying through to a position of peace (Philippians 4: 6, 7). In others it's a matter of praying until we know that we've arrived at a position of complete submission to God's will, however He chooses to answer our prayers (Matthew 26: 39-44; cf 2 Corinthians 12: 7-10). In any matter which gives rise to anxiety or conflict, aim to pray through to submission and peace - both are necessary, and in that order.

Practical Prayer

'How do I know if my faith is sufficient when I pray? And is it contrary to faith "to put out a fleece" to God in prayer?'

It's extremely difficult to measure faith. Our feelings may let us down so that we minimise the real gift of faith God has given us. On the other hand, we may fall into the snare of exaggerating the extent of our faith. The Lord Jesus spoke of the importance and value of faith no matter how small it may be - faith as small as a mustard seed has the power to move mountains (Matthew 17: 20). And the incident which prompted Jesus to say this was the healing of the epileptic, whose father had cried, 'I do believe; help me overcome my unbelief!' (Mark 9: 24).

Our faith is sufficient if we come with boldness and assurance to God in the name of His Son, if we wrestle in prayer honestly with our doubts - when we have them - and if we discover peace at the end. Far more important than the sufficiency of our faith is the sufficiency of the God in whom we have faith, through His Son Jesus Christ.

The better question to ask, therefore, is 'How may I strengthen my faith when I feel that it's weak?' and the answer to this is straightforward. First and foremost, we must focus our attention - the eyes of our soul - on God Himself, and especially as He has made Himself known to us in the Lord Jesus Christ. Hudson Taylor, the founder of the China Inland Mission, went through a great crisis of faith which had much to do with his confidence in God and his practice of prayer. A turning point was the help he received from words passed on to him in a letter from a friend:

'How then to have our faith increased? Only by thinking of all that Jesus *is* , and all He is *for us* : His life, His death, His work, He Himself as revealed to us in the Word, to be the subject of our constant thoughts. Not a striving to have faith, or to increase our faith, but a looking off to the Faithful One seems all we need; a

120

resting in the Loved One entirely, for time and for eternity. It does not appear to me as anything new, only formerly misapprehended.'

When we grasp the truth of our Lord Jesus Christ's sufficiency, faith rises to lay hold of that sufficiency.

If we feel we are praying unbelievingly, three questions may be profitably asked: 'Is this a right request I'm making to God?' 'Is it in accord with God's character?' and 'Does my unbelief arise because I'm not sure of the answer to one or other of these questions?' If I can answer a clear 'Yes' to either of the first two questions, then I must deliberately raise the shield of faith against Satan's fiery darts of doubt and unbelief (Ephesians 6: 16). If, however, the answer is 'No', then my unbelief isn't surprising, and I need to double check the reasons for my request.

The idea of putting out a fleece comes from the story of Gideon in Judges 6: 36-40 when he wanted proof that it was really God who was calling him to lead his people against the Midianites. There's no suggestion at all that Gideon was to be commended in this, or that it should be a pattern we should follow. In fact, there was an element of unbelief or doubt behind Gideon's practice. But God was gracious to Gideon in his weakness as He is to us.

There are times when we desperately need direction, and sometimes in situations where there's no direct instruction in the Bible. Let's imagine that a person is in the happy position of applying for two jobs, with the likelihood of both being offered him. Assured of God's control of everything, I believe it would be right to pray that the first job offered to him might be the one God has chosen, in so far as it wouldn't be honourable to accept one, and then before ever beginning it, to reject it because the second one was also offered, with perhaps more attractive terms.

I can think of a couple of occasions recently where I've wanted confirmation of the rightness or otherwise of a course of action I've had in mind, but I've been anxious in case I haven't been seeing the situation right. After prayer I've decided to share the matters - in one case with a friend and the other with my wife - telling God beforehand that whatever their reaction was, I would see that as the confirmation or rejection of what I had in mind. In one case my proposed course of action wasn't confirmed and in the other it was; but I've complete peace that God's answer was given me in both cases.

I would be cautious in putting out a fleece if the grounds were really unbelief on my part; but if it arises from an earnest desire not to step out of God's will, and I need some confirmation of His guidance, I believe I may look for the signs which I feel are appropriate. But situations like this should be the exception rather than the rule.

'How do I know if I'm fervent enough in my prayers?'
The question is prompted by the attention James draws to Elijah's fervency or earnestness in prayer (James 5: 16-18). Earnestness is probably a better word than fervency. We may tend to measure fervency by how we think we sound when we pray. With some of us fervency of spirit - and that's what really counts - may find natural expression in fervency of speech but that's not the case with all of us. The question itself may indicate that we're looking at ourselves as we pray more than we ought.

Obvious tests of fervency may be applied. We're fervent when we don't pray vaguely but specifically. We're fervent when we persist in praying for what we believe is right and God-honouring, no matter how great the difficulties or the waiting period. We're fervent when we look for God's answer after we've prayed.

How may I know that I'm praying in the will of God? How do I distinguish between God's desires and my own desires?'

To say I know that on every occasion when I pray I do so in God's will would be presumptuous. When we pray for general and fundamental matters - such as those illustrated in the Lord's Prayer - we know that we're praying in God's will. But when we come to specific details, perhaps in the application of those fundamentals, we may not be as sure. So, for example, I can pray with confidence every day and on every occasion, 'Hallowed be Your Name!" But in some crisis-situation in the local Church, when perhaps there's the danger of God's Name being dishonoured by the bad behaviour of God's people, I may not know exactly how to pray. My safety, however, is to pray, 'Hallowed be Your Name!' and to present myself as a willing instrument in God's hands for the achieving of this.

Prayer for healing in a case of serious illness is the kind of situation which prompts us to ask, 'Am I praying in God's will? Am I simply expressing my own desires or God's will?' Our own desires, while perhaps naturally suspect because of our fallen natures, are not to be despised. Hopefully, the more we grow in grace and in the knowledge of God, the more our desires will be influenced and moulded by our knowledge of God, and of His will. Personally, I feel that when the matters we pray about relate to health and life expectancy, unless God lays a burden upon us to the contrary, we should generally pray that God's will may be done for the person concerned, that God will be his comfort and strength, and that God's good purposes will be worked out through the illness.

A number of things help me to know that I pray in God's will. I pray in God's will as I ask Him honestly for the wisdom to know how to pray for the person or matter which I feel to be urgent. I may know that I pray in God's will as I begin by submitting myself to His will, whatever it may be, in the matter about which I pray. I pray in God's will as I relate my praying as carefully as I know how to what God has revealed in the Bible about His will. And I pray in God's will when my major and predominating concern is God's honour and glory, without the presumption on my part of thinking that I always know best how He may be glorified.

'What should I do about problems of concentration?'
Many problems of concentration arise from lack of method in prayer, and not having some form of prayer diary. Sometimes the problem is that we're not really thinking about what we're doing, and we're praying out of habit, without earnestness. We know we ought to pray but we're not coming to God with definite things we want from Him. Martin Luther had a puppy by the name of Tolpel. When Luther sat at the table for a meal the dog watched with open mouth and motionless eyes. Luther drew a lesson from it. 'Oh, if I could only pray the way this dog watches the meat! All his thoughts are concentrated on the piece of meat. Otherwise he has no thought, wish or hope.' The first thing to check out is our earnestness.

The problem may be one of tiredness or physical posture. If you're tired and you kneel at your bed to pray, you may lose concentration and even fall asleep. I find it helps concentration to walk around, or even to go for a walk in order to pray without the distractions that there may often be in the home.

Sometimes our major problem is that as we begin to pray - feeling that we must first praise and thank God - other things burst in upon our mind. Our mind becomes like a butterfly, moving from one subject to another. The most effective remedy is to pray immediately about the matters that are distracting your attention. Let's imagine you begin to pray, aiming to follow your usual pattern of worship, praise and thanksgiving. As soon as you begin to pray, your concentration goes because you are thinking of a difficult interview you have at two o'clock in the afternoon, and you've a problem with a leaking roof that's got to be sorted out. You push these things out of your mind, and pray. But they come back again. How are you going to cope with the interview? Which builder should you go to for help? The answer is to pray for the interview in detail there and then, to ask for God's help in the practical matter of the roof, and then to return to your praise and worship of God. In fact, your praise and worship of God will be all the more meaningful because you'll have appreciated afresh how practical and real God's fatherly concern for you is. Chase the distractions by praying about them, and concentration will usually take care of itself.

'How should I think about my prayers that God doesn't answer?'
To answer this question we have to think first of those things which may disqualify our prayers' acceptance, and then, second, of those situations where our prayers are genuine and acceptable but *appear* to receive no answer.

Unanswered prayer may sometimes be the result of our having offered the wrong kind of prayer. A basic condition of prayer is that our requests must be in keeping with God's nature, so that they please Him and are in harmony with His will (1 John 5: 14). Prayers offered with wrong motives and for the wrong things are unanswered, for, as James writes, 'When you ask, you do not receive, because you ask with wrong motives, that you may spend what you get on your pleasures' (James 4: 3). Prayers offered when we are living in disobedience to God are likely to be unanswered (1 John 3: 21, 22) and prayer that is merely offered with our lips is not really prayer at all (Isaiah 1: 15f; 29: 13).

But the real problem often arises when we pray what we believe are correct prayers and they seem to be without their answer. At this point we may be dogmatic and say that such prayers are never unanswered. That's not a 'get-out' but a fact. Our Father always hears our requests, and He always gives His answer - but 'No' is as much an answer as 'Yes'. Looking back over my happy relationship with my father, I thank God for the love he showed me and the care he had for me. He gave me many things, and he responded to my many requests, especially when I was younger. But sometimes he said, 'No'.

I admit that we don't always understand God's 'Nos'. There's the lovely story of Dr W E Sangster when he was a boy away at boarding school. Short of money he sent a crisp message home: 'SOS, LSD, RSVP.' He waited patiently for his father's expected reply. His friends commiserated with him. 'Your father's forgotten you,' was their suggestion. This he vigorously rejected. 'When I get home,' he said, 'I'll ask him.'

We really need to want God to say 'No' to some of our prayers. Elijah, in a state of desperation, cried, 'I have had enough, Lord. Take my life' (1 Kings 19: 4). Mercifully, God didn't answer his prayer. Sometimes the worst thing that could happen is that God should answer our prayers, for what we want may be detrimental to us (see Numbers 11: 4, 33 and Psalm 106: 13-15).

The particular problem we have with regard to 'unanswered prayer' may be over prayer for someone's physical healing in the light of verses like Matthew 18: 19, 20: 'Again, I tell you that if two of you on earth agree about anything you ask for, it will be done for you by my Father in heaven. For where two or three come together in my name, there am I with them.' But bear in mind there's always a danger of taking a verse either out of its context or of not looking at it in relation to what the Bible says elsewhere on the same subject. Clearly what Jesus says in verse 19 must be qualified in some way - He's not giving blanket approval to anything we might choose to ask. Jesus makes this promise in the context of Church life and about matters which may threaten the good name of the

Church, and therefore the honour of God's Name (see verses 15-18). Furthermore, the two verses clearly go together, and the key factor is that Christians come together in Jesus' Name, and - by implication - pray in His Name. To pray in Jesus' Name is to pray for that which will bring glory to His Name. What we must accept - when it comes to prayer for healing - is that He may be glorified in a Christian's death as in his healing.

The fact that we and others may pray for the healing of a Christian friend isn't positive proof that it's God's will to heal him. We may sometimes pray beyond our understanding - and God knows that, and is gracious in answering our prayers in the way that's best. We've already pointed out that submission to God's will - before we know what His will is - should be a starting point of prayer. I should certainly pray according to my convictions, but I must never be so presumptuous as to say that my convictions are always God-given. I would give much more weight, however, to the shared and united convictions that God gives to the elders or spiritual leaders of a Church who are called in by an unwell person to pray for him, for the New Testament teaches that God may give them the gift of faith to know exactly what to ask (James 5: 14, 15).

In many of the things for which we pray - especially where we feel our prayers have been 'unanswered' - we're inclined to be much too time-conscious or impatient. Adoniram Judson, who served as a missionary in Burma at the beginning of the nineteenth century, testified, 'I never prayed sincerely and earnestly for anything but it came; at some time - no matter how distant the day - somehow in some shape, probably the last I should have devised, it came.'

To be realistic

We need to be realistic about our problems and questions about prayer.

First, we'll never have all the answers this side of heaven, but that should not stop us praying. Prayer is asking, but it's far more than asking - it's a most precious means of developing our friendship with God.

Second, our use of prayer - both as a boon and as a weapon - tends to be weak because we're weak. Nevertheless, it remains the greatest support in our weakness, and our strongest defence against the devil's attacks upon our weakness.

Finally, our confidence in prayer isn't in our understanding of it, or our methods or discipline in it, but in God's character and revelation of Himself in our Lord Jesus Christ. The one true God has become our Father through the gift of His glorious Son. 'What, then, shall we say in response to this? If God is for us, who can be against us? He who did not spare his own Son, but gave him up for us all - how will he not also, along with him, graciously give us all things?' (Romans 8: 31, 32).

A prayer

Father in heaven, I thank You that the things I know about prayer far exceed the things I don't know. I thank You that I know that You are my Father, that Your Son, the Lord Jesus, is my Saviour and Lord, and that Your Holy Spirit is my Counsellor. I know that all Your promises are totally reliable and true.

Teach me to be honest with myself and with You when I have difficulties and questions so that where You want to give me greater understanding I may find it, and that where You want me to wait and trust You I may be patient. I ask this in Your Son's Name. Amen.